FROM COMMON SCHOOL TO MAGNET SCHOOL

Lectures Delivered for the
National Endowment for the Humanities
Boston Public Library
Learning Library Program

FROM COMMON SCHOOL TO MAGNET SCHOOL

Selected Essays in the History of Boston's Schools

Edited by
JAMES W. FRASER,
HENRY L. ALLEN, and
SAM BARNES

Boston, Trustees of the Public Library
of the City of Boston, 1979

Library of Congress Cataloging in Publication Data
Main entry under title:

From Common School to Magnet School.

Bibliography: p.
Includes index.
1. Education—Massachusetts—Boston—History—Addresses, essays,
lectures. 2. School integration—Massachusetts—Boston—History—
Addresses, essays, lectures. 3. Catholic Church in Boston—Education—
History—Addresses, essays, lectures. I. Fraser, James W., 1944-
II. Allen, Henry L., 1942- III. Barnes, Nancy, 1946- IV. Series: Boston
Public Library. National Endowment for the Humanities Learning Library
Program.

Library of Congress Cataloging in Publication Data

Humanities Learning Library Program, Boston Public Library; no. 8.
LA306.B7F76 370'.9744'61 78-31337
ISBN 0-89073-059-8

Illustration Credits

28. Horace Mann. Courtesy of Kent State University Press.
63. The Most Reverend John J. Williams, Archbishop of Boston.
Courtesy of the Pilot Publishing Co.
71. St. Thomas Aquinas parish, Jamaica Plain.
Courtesy of St. Thomas Aquinas parish.
76. Fresh air school, Boston. Courtesy of the Library of Congress.
79. Pauline Agassiz Shaw. Courtesy of the Boston Globe.
83. Manual Training for girls in a Boston School.
Courtesy of the Library of Congress.
86. North Bennett Street Industrial School. Courtesy of the Boston Globe.
92. Boston public school classroom, 1917. Courtesy of the Library of Congress.
108. Ellen Jackson. Courtesy of the Boston Globe.
117. Operation Exodus bus. Courtesy of the Boston Globe.
120. 1974 march following desegregation order. Courtesy of the Boston Globe.
123. Black students leave South Boston High School.
Courtesy of World Wide Photos.
128. The William Monroe Trotter School in Roxbury.
Courtesy of the Boston Globe.

CONTENTS

To the Parents and Students of Boston's Public Schools, Past, Present, and Future.

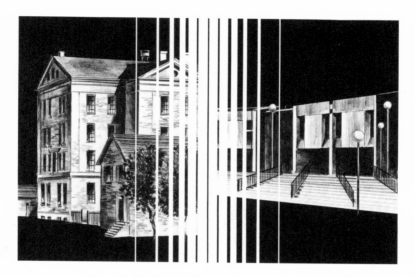

Since 1974 attention has focused to an unparalleled extent on the crisis in Boston's public schools. Court-ordered integration has brought to the surface a wide variety of concerns about the quality of education in the city's schools, the importance of the neighborhood school, the place of various racial and ethnic groups in school policy, and ultimately the value of a publicly supported and publicly controlled school system for a large urban area. The current crisis is unique, but many of these issues have been faced, in slightly different form perhaps, by previous generations of Bostonians. In this context the National Endowment for the Humanities' Learning Library Program at the Boston Public Library chose the history of Boston's schools as a subject of particular interest around which study ought to be organized. The result was the presentation of a series of lectures at the Library in February and March 1977, the production of a bibliography, and now this publication of a revised form of the lectures themselves. It is our hope that the published lectures will make available to a larger audience material that is of interest and indeed important for the future of Boston.

Living as it does in the midst of numerous universities, Boston and its educational system have been the subject of numerous doctoral dissertations, monographs, and other studies. But no one has written a complete or definitive history of the system. Some decades and incidents have been interpreted and reinterpreted; others, especially in the early twentieth century, have been virtually ignored. One of the frustrations that all of the authors of this study have faced has been the plethora of materials on some phases of our work and the near total absence of materials in others. The full history of Boston's schools is yet to be written. This book should be considered as an interim report by a number of people who are continuing to work on Boston's educational history. Perhaps it can be a spur to more complete work in the future.

Our primary concern in this book is to focus on certain key events and issues, which will help readers gain an understanding of the forces and personalities that have brought the current situation in Boston's schools into existence. We hope to provide a resource that will help all of us—parents, teachers, and concerned citizens—understand more clearly and perhaps more humanely the developments that have brought us to the present. Without some knowledge of where our schools have been, it is indeed difficult to imagine an intelligent move into the future. We hope that our essays will help Bostonians consider carefully the alternatives open to them.

The book has been planned and edited by the three people who took initial responsibility for the lecture series— James Fraser, Henry Allen, and Sam Barnes. We were pleased that two others—Byron Rushing and James Sanders—were willing to join us in the teaching and writing, sharing their special fields of expertise as essays in this story. We wish to thank the many others who have helped make this book possible: Patricia Graham, formerly of the Radcliffe Institute and now the Director of the National Institute of Education, for making the first contacts between the library and the editors, the Church of the Covenant, Boston, for giving Mr. Fraser time to do much of the editing, the *Boston Globe* for a grant to Ms. Barnes to work on these essays; George Collins of the *Boston Globe* library for help with the photographs, and Sharlene Vest of Boston College for sharing her unpublished

research on Superintendent Jeremiah Burke. We are espe-   ix
cially grateful to the very helpful staff members of the Boston
Public Library for their support, encouragement, and prod-
ding, especially Paul Wright who coordinated the lectures,
offered suggestions, and provided the title, and Diane Kleiner
and Rick Zonghi who coordinated the editing and publication. James Breeden of the Boston Public Schools reviewed
the text and provided numerous suggestions as the manuscript
was edited, and Kay Allen helped with much of the typing.
Responsibility for the content of each essay, including unfortunately errors in fact or interpretation, rests, of course, with
its author.

CHAPTER 1

Boston's Colonial and Revolutionary Experience, 1629–1819

JAMES W. FRASER

The famous *New England Primer* served as the primary textbook for Boston's colonial schools and well illustrates the dual concern for literacy and religious orthodoxy.

2   Boston was settled in 1629 by Puritans from England. These religious dissidents came not for the principle of religious freedom but for the freedom to practice what they saw as the only true religion—their own. In the wilderness of the New World—they did not count native Americans—they hoped to show the rest of the world what true religion and a good society could be. Puritans were one party within the Church of England that had itself recently broken from Rome and was still seeking its own position within the spectrum of Protestantism. Because they wanted to push the Reformation further than their coreligionists did, the Puritans often came into conflict with the authorities in England, and so a group of them moved to the New World. They did not necessarily come with the idea that they would spend their whole lives in New England, but as John Winthrop, their governor, described their mission, they wanted to set up "a city upon a hill," that the eyes of the rest of the world might be upon them. They especially hoped that old England would see their success and be transformed in the New England model.

One important part of the model society for these English Puritans was good schools. They came to Boston at a time when schools in England were probably better than they had ever been before, or would be again for another two centuries: they were open to more people, there were more of them, and they were more widely dispersed. This does not mean that the vast majority of English youth went to school, but sometime in the late 1400s and 1500s in England, schools were open to many boys and to some girls to provide the beginnings of education in both English and Latin (Latin being the language necessary to study what people considered the great literature).

Five years after the settlement in Boston, the records of the town indicate that "our brother, Philemon Pormont, shall be entreated to become schoolmaster for the teaching and nurturing of children with us."[1] That was April 13, 1635, as good a date as any other for the first school in Boston. Charlestown adopted a similar resolution the next year.

---

1) Quoted in Lawrence A. Cremin, *American Education: The Colonial Experience* (New York: Harper & Row, 1970), p. 180.

Within a decade both Dorchester and Roxbury, which were
separate settlements, had adopted similar resolutions.

The model of schooling that was imported for Boston
had three stages. At the beginning were English schools, sometimes called petty schools, for relatively young children, usually
both boys and girls, which taught basic English reading, some
writing, some arithmetic, and the beginnings of English literature—at least enough so that children could read the Bible
and the catechism, which was, after all, the essential literature
in the Puritans' view. The next level was the Latin grammar
school. It covered a seven-year curriculum—normally started
by children about seven years old—teaching Latin grammar
from an elementary to a fairly advanced level, and introductory
Greek and Hebrew for those who were interested in the ministry. The grammar school had one purpose: preparation for
college. Because college instruction in England at Oxford and
Cambridge and in Boston at Harvard College (established in
1636) was in Latin, students had to study the language to be
admitted.

Within a decade of the first settlement, between 1630
and 1640, Boston had set up all three stages of that ideal
English schooling system: English school, Latin school, and
college. Pormont, the first schoolmaster, carried on instruction in both an English school and in a Latin grammar school,
and across the river in Cambridge, Henry Dunster was opening what became Harvard College. The system was established, though it did not always function quite as smoothly as
some of its founders would have liked. Pormont himself left
the colony a year after he was appointed because he was found
guilty of heresy; he had supported Ann Hutchinson, a religious rebel, against the religious leaders. Daniel Maud was
elected to succeed him. Following Maud a variety of Latin
schoolmasters, mostly young Harvard graduates who hoped to
become ministers, spent a year or two as schoolmaster while
they waited for a parish.

In 1645 Boston built a schoolhouse. Thus one of these
dates—either 1635 when Pormont was appointed or 1645—
can be considered the starting date for the Boston Latin
School. From that date to the present, Latin grammar has
been taught in the city of Boston. While the other subjects

For its first ten years of existence, the Boston Latin School met in the homes of its successive masters. In 1645, however, the town built its first school building to house the instruction.

taught, the location and the means of instruction have changed many times over the past three and one half centuries, one can argue without stretching the point too far, that there has been a Boston Latin School for all of that time.

At the same time that the Puritans were setting up schools, they were also passing laws to make sure that education did in fact take place. The first charter reform around school legislation took place in 1642 when the legislature of the commonwealth of Massachusetts adopted a law that parents and masters of indentured servants were required to teach their children or servants "to read and understand the principles of religion and the capital lawes of the country."[2] The law also required that these children must be constantly employed in some useful occupation, a theme that has appeared in every generation since then.

From the first school law to the present, the purposes of education have been mixed; they include both concern that children be able to read and also that they be kept out of trouble. In different ways at different times, the purpose of educa-

2) Quoted in Samuel Eliot Morison, *The Intellectual Life of Colonial New England* (Ithaca: Cornell University Press, 1936, 1956), p. 66.

tion has also been to keep people orthodox, though the definition of orthodoxy has changed over the years. Whatever the purposes, the school laws were impressive. Fifteen years after the first white settlement in Boston, a law had been passed requiring that every parent assume responsibility that their child could read and know the principles of religion and the capital laws of the country.

In 1647, the legislature again took up school matters and passed a more comprehensive education law. Its preamble includes one of the more oft-quoted statements in educational history.

It being one chief project of that old deluder, Satan, to keep men from the knowledge of Scripture, as in former times by keeping them in an unknown tongue, . . . that learning may not be buried in the grave of our fathers in the church and commonwealth, the Lord assisting our endeavors. . . . It is therefore ordered, that every township in this jurisdiction, after the Lord hath increased them to the number of fifty householders, shall then forthwith appoint one within their own town to teach all such children as shall resort to him to write and read, whose wages shall be paid either by the parents or masters of such children, or by those inhabitants in general, . . . and it is further ordered, that where any town shall increase up to the number of one hundred families or householders they shall set up a grammar school, the master thereof being able to instruct youth so far as they may be fitted for the university."[3]

By the time the law was adopted, Boston already had well over the one hundred families. Unlike many of the other towns in the commonwealth, Boston always complied with the law. The schools always offered English and Latin instruction to prepare students for the university.

By 1650 a Boston schoolboy—I use the term advisedly—had the opportunity to attend English school, Latin grammar school, and, across the river, a full college course. At the same time the legal system required all parents to make

---

3) Cremin, *American Education*, pp. 181–182.

sure that their children, female and male, learned to read at least well enough to know the basic documents of the society.

For the next century, Boston continued to operate its school system in about the same form. The school laws did not require use of the school system, however; they merely required that a child learn to read and that the schools be available. How an individual child met the standard was completely up to the family. And for the vast majority of children, other methods, or a combination of some schooling with other methods, met both the legal requirements and the hopes and needs of child and parent.

That quintessential Bostonian, Benjamin Franklin, provides a useful example of how the Boston system operated in reality. When Franklin set out to attend school in the early 1700s, he planned to use the system for his own ends. He described the experience in his autobiography:

> My older brothers were all put out apprentices to different trades. I was put to the grammar school at eight years of age, my father intending to devote me as the tithe of his sons in the service of the church. My early readiness in learning to read . . . and the opinion of his friends that I should certainly make a good scholar [Franklin at no time in his life was a humble person], encouraged my father in this purpose of his. . . . I continued, however, at the grammar school rather less than a year though in that time I had risen gradually from the middle of the class of that year to be at the head of the same class. . . . But my father burdened with a numerous family and unable without inconvenience to support the expense of a college education, considering moreover as he said to one of his friends in my presence, the little encouragement that line of life afforded to those educated for it [Franklin and his father were both agreeing that Franklin would not make a very good preacher] . . . gave up his first intentions, took me from the grammar school, and sent me to a school for writing and arithmetic, kept by the then famous man, Mr. Geo. Brownell. He was a skillful mas-

ter and successful in his profession, employing the
mildest and most encouraging methods. Under him I
learned to write a good hand pretty soon, but I failed at
arithmetic and made no progress in it. At ten years old I
was taken home to help my father in his business.[4]

Instead of moving from English school to grammar
school to college, Franklin started out in grammar school
because he could already read and was preparing himself for
Latin grammar to move on to college. For a variety of reasons,
Franklin and his father decided that this arrangement was not
a good idea after all, so Franklin gave up on grammar school
after a year and went back to an English school. Although he
could read, he also wanted to learn writing and arithmetic.
He spent one year in elementary school and picked up, as he
describes it, not much arithmetic but some writing. Then he
dropped out of the Boston schools altogether.

Some at Boston Latin School still refer to Franklin as
one of their proud graduates. He is instead one of their proud
dropouts. And he is far more typical of the vast majority of the
people who attended the schools in Boston than anyone who
moved properly through the system. For modern Americans
who live with a school system that is set up for people to move
from kindergarten through first grade right on through twelfth
grade, it is hard to conceive of the flexibility that existed in
colonial institutions. There was a pattern, but people used the
institutions as they found them functional. If they were, in
fact, preparing for college, they would attend grammar
school. If they were preparing for a career in the trades, they
might attend the English schools long enough to learn the
necessary arithmetic to engage in their work. The vast majority of Bostonians never attended the schools at all. Girls were
not welcome, particularly in the Latin schools. They were
accepted in the English schools, but most of them, along with
their brothers, learned to read at home.

Instruction in the schools probably began with the
famous hornbook, a sheet of wood covered with horn that

---

4) Benjamin Franklin, *The Autobiography of Benjamin Franklin* (New York: New
American Library, 1961), pp. 22–23.

8   showed the alphabet and a few sentences. From here the child would proceed to a primer, from which the catechism and other basic reading might be learned. Sometime around 1690, one of the most popular books in the annals of education, the *New England Primer*, became available and remained the staple text in schools until the time of the Revolution. Beginning with the alphabet—from "In Adam's Fall We Sinned All" to "Zacheus he Did climb the Tree His Lord to see,"—the child learned to read and to understand the basis of Puritan morality at the same time.

   With the Puritan or Congregational church as the established religion of the colony, there was no serious challenge to the religious tone of the text. The separation of religion from schooling was far in the future. The child's duties to family, church, and society were the same, and they were learned as one learned to read from the primer:

   I will fear God, and Honour the King.
   I will honour my Father & Mother.
   I will Obey my Superiours.
   I will Submit to my Elders.
   I will Love my Friends.
   I will hate no Man.
   I will forgive my Enemies, and pray to God for them.
   I will as much as in me lies keep all God's Holy
      Commandments.[5]

   Even after the Revolution, a slightly secularized and highly republicanized version of the primer continued in use. While mention of the king disappeared and *W* was changed from "Whales in the Sea God's Voice obey" to "Great Washington brave His country Did Save," the primer continued for another generation.

   The schools had been set up by order of the state legislature, but control of their administration and content rested with the town. In Boston, the Board of Selectmen set the budget and inspected the schools. In 1710, however, a special

---

5) *The New England Primer Enlarged. For the More Easy Attaining the True Reading of English. To Which Is Added, The Assembly of Divines Catechism* (Boston: S. Kneeland & T. Green, 1727), ed. Paul Leicester Ford (New York: Dodd, Mead, 1897). (Paperback: Teachers College Press, 1962).

five-member board of visitors was appointed to visit the five
schools and report periodically. They were perhaps the first
example of what would become a powerful American institution
—the board of education.

The American Revolution disrupted schools in Massachusetts as it did throughout the rest of the nation. All of
Boston's schools were closed at the height of the war, and
many were slow to reopen. After the war, political independence meant that a new government, including new govern-
ance for the schools, had to be devised. The new state constitution of 1780 stressed the importance of schools "to
contenance and inculcate the principles of humanity and
general benevolence, public and private charity, industry and
frugality, honesty and punctuality, . . . sincerity, good humor,
and all social affections, generous sentiments, among the people."[6] The probable author of those lines, John Adams, had
been campaigning for some time for an expanded public
school system. He was committed to the system for many reasons. At best Adams, the revolutionary, believed in equal
opportunity for all, and as he worked to build an equal and just
commonwealth, he demanded the equalizing of opportunity
that good schools would give. At the same time Adams, the
aristocrat, was afraid to walk down the streets of his native
Boston while "my eyes are so diverted with Chimney Sweeps,
Carriers of Wood, Merchants, Ladies, Priests, Carts, Horses,
Oxen, Coaches, Market men and Women, Soldiers, Sailors,
and my Ears with the Rattle Gabble of them all that I can't
think long enough in the Street upon any one Thing to start
and pursue a Thought."[7] The solution to this confusion, the
return to a simpler, quieter, more virtuous Boston where the
Adamses were respected, could lie through a school system in
which the "principles of humanity and general benevolence
. : . industry and frugality, honesty and punctuality" were all
inculcated. This mixture of motives—supporting schools

---

6) Quoted by Stanley K. Schultz, *The Culture Factory: Boston Public Schools,
1789–1860* (New York: Oxford University Press, 1973), pp. 8–9. The early sections of these lectures are deeply indebted to Schultz's detailed account of the rise
of the Boston school system.

7) Ibid.

10 because they will benefit all children and supporting schools because they will protect the lives and property of the reformers—has surfaced in every subsequent generation of school reformers.

Following the new constitution, the state legislature in 1789 passed a school law reaffirming many of the colonial regulations. Every town had to support an elementary school; larger ones also had to have a grammar school; and the budgets would be set through the town meeting.

A few months later, the Boston town meeting focused again on schools and appointed a committee of twelve to draft a plan for a new school system. John Adams believed that the schools should be open to all but should be controlled by the wise and the good. His more radical cousin, Sam Adams, was less sure than John who the wise and the good were and therefore argued that in fact the schools should be controlled by the whole community. Sam Adams was able to defeat his cousin in the elections for the special committee, which would draw up the system, and Sam's proposals were adopted by the town meeting in September 1789. The purpose of the new system, as recommended by Sam Adams and his committee, was to

John and Sam Adams, cousins who jointly supported the American revolution, but disagreed about most of the details, including how the schools of the newly independent nation should be run.

create a more organized system. The previous one had been organized in theory, but in fact there had been private schools, public schools, apprenticeship, all merging together, and people like Ben Franklin moving in and out. Boston, now setting up its new commonwealth, wanted to order this new system and change control of it. The recommendations of this committee, which were adopted, did several things for the Boston schools. First, they assigned one of the schools to teach Latin grammar by itself. Thus Boston Latin was reaffirmed as the school for college preparation. Three other schools within the city system were to teach English grammar, writing, and arithmetic. The same ordinance officially opened the English schools to girls as well as boys. In fact some schools had been opened to girls prior to this, but the law had simply been silent on this matter. Now the law said that the English schools were open to girls as well as boys for the half of the school year during the summer when the boys were busy in the fields. It also established regular school hours: 7:30 until 11 in the morning and 2 to 5 in the afternoon. It raised the age of entrance to Boston Latin School to ten to encourage everyone to attend the English schools and to get a broader mix of people in the English schools. It also replaced the *New England Primer* with a book being written by Noah Webster, which was first used in Massachusetts and would become a dominant textbook in much of the United States. The book was a more secularized and more patriotic version than the primer, introducing the ideas of the American Revolution into the school curriculum. The final reform we still have with us: Sam Adams' committee set up the Boston School Committee. Twelve members, one from each of the twelve wards of the city, were elected to control the school system. The purpose of the school committee as it was set up in 1789 was to separate control of the schools from the rest of the city government. The school committee would be accountable to the people, and would set the school budget, and control operations and the curriculum.

One other provision in the 1789 system limited its usefulness. A child had to be able to read English before he or she could be admitted to the English schools. The school system would help improve reading ability. It would teach writing

12   and arithmetic and give enough instruction in English litera-
      ture so that one could be admitted to grammar school, but it
      would not teach basic reading. Basic reading was to be learned
      privately either at home or in the so-called dame school where
      a woman would teach reading to half a dozen students for
      some minimal fee. It was not assumed at this point to be the
      responsibility of the state to teach that basic skill.

     The Adams' reforms set the basic structure of Boston's
public schools. Some, such as the elected school committee,
have survived to the present; others were changed drastically
over the years. But for several decades, almost no additional
changes were made. The colonial system had been regularized
and democratized. It would take a new generation to go further.

     As the new system began to operate, three issues
quickly came to the fore. One had been raised even before the
reforms but had been ignored by the reformers. In 1787
Boston, with a population of twenty thousand, had a black
population of about eight hundred. The black parents petitioned the legislature requesting schools for their children and
stating that they paid taxes but received no benefit from the
schools of Boston. The legislature denied the petition. In
1798 black parents turned to the city requesting schools for
their children. The selectmen denied the request. In 1800 the
black parents petitioned the newly formed school committee
for a separate school for black children saying that black children were either excluded or not given equal opportunity
within the existing schools. The school committee refused
their request. This is the beginning of an issue that has grown
in importance with each generation. Boston first developed a
separate black school system in the early 1800s and then
began the long struggle for the integration of that system into
the one used by most of the rest of Boston's children. It is
indeed ironic that in the same decade as the initial establishment of the Boston School Committee, the issue of segregated schools and lack of opportunity in the Boston schools
for the small free black population of the city was being
raised.

     The second issue that emerged was the establishment
by Protestant reformers of Sunday schools for those children

who were working all week and therefore were not able to use
the public schools. The schools, which began to appear soon after 1789, did not teach any more religious subjects than were offered in the public schools at first. They did, however, provide instruction for those children who worked all week and could not attend public school during the five days of the week. They functioned that way for a short period of time and were then transformed into the institution more or less that we know today—a religious adjunct to the public school system to provide specialized religious training on Sunday for the children who were in the public schools the rest of the week.

The third issue which began to create tensions almost as soon as the new system started operation was the requirement that a child had to be able to read to get into the system. Fairly quickly after the system began to operate, parents began to object. If they were having trouble teaching their children to read and could not afford to send them to a private instructor, they were unable to use the system that their tax money was supporting. Boston was not anxious to respond to that need, and it was not until 1817 that a petition was presented to the town meeting signed by a fairly large number of parents, requesting the schools to teach reading. The town meeting responded as governments have to many other issues ever since; it set up a commission to examine the issue. The study commission was surprised at what it learned. The eight public schools in the city served approximately twenty-three hundred children, about 16 percent of those eligible. There were 154 private schools in the city serving close to four thousand children who were paying to learn either basic reading or more advanced skills in some other context. Eight charity schools provided free instruction to another four hundred or so children. There were still—and the study commission was unable to figure out how to count them—significant numbers of children who were excluded or for one reason or another were not part of this system.

In 1818, the petition came back to the town meeting to set up a system of primary schools to teach basic literacy, and it opened a major debate. A number of parents supported the system. Some of the prestigious leaders of the community—William Ellery Channing, who was launching his career as a

14   famous Unitarian minister, and Thomas Dawes, who rode with Paul Revere—supported the parents. Harrison Gray Otis, a leading citizen, led the opposition. "Let us eschew the vagaries and notions of new schools," Otis asserted.[8] The new proposal would be expensive, and the old was good enough. In spite of his rhetoric, Otis lost. The town meeting voted to accept the petition and set up a Primary School Board subservient to the main school committee, although fairly independent, and it appropriated $5,000 to set up twenty schools to teach reading and to rescue children from the vice of the streets. The schools were opened within two years. A fixed set of money was paid to the teacher, usually a woman, who would find quarters for providing the instruction. Often the teacher set aside a room of his or her home as the classroom. By 1820, there were thirty-four primary schools along with the eight grammar schools, which together served about 25 percent of the eligible children.

     With a population of forty-three thousand in 1820, Boston remained a small, relatively homogeneous city. The black population was about seventeen hundred (4 percent). No significant new immigrant groups had yet arrived. The Anglo-Saxon stock that had settled Boston two centuries before remained the dominant ethnic component. The next decades would see all of this change rapidly. Between 1820 and 1850, the population would grow to 136,000. Most of these newcomers represented new ethnic groups, especially the Irish. By their economic poverty and cultural differences, they did not fit easily into the city's institutions, and by their sheer numbers, they made the administration of the schools far more complex. The story of schooling in Boston in the first half of the nineteenth century is one of change beyond the wildest expectations of those who had so carefully laid the basis of the system through the reforms of 1819. Yet that basis remained and was used to educate children for many years.

---

8) Ibid, p. 40.

CHAPTER 2

Black Schools in White Boston, 1800–1860

BYRON RUSHING

Boston's first segregated school.

16   During September 1974—the beginning of the implementation of the court-ordered plan to desegregate Boston's public schools—the Museum of Afro American History mounted an exhibit, "Integration! 1855," on black education in Boston in the nineteenth century. The year 1855 marked the successful completion of the struggle of Afro-American and white abolitionists in Massachusetts to end public school segregation. It was the high point in the 19th century struggle for quality education for black children in Boston.

To understand what happened in 1855 we must go back to the beginnings of Afro-American history in Boston. Although there are some vague references to Africans in Massachusetts before 1637, the following incidents of 1637–1638 are the first to be clearly documented. They form a fascinating paradigm of subsequent race relations in the United States. In 1637 some of the native Americans south of the Shawmut peninsula realized that life with the English was not to be an everlasting Thanksgiving. War broke out, and the Pequod Indians lost. The surviving Indians—prisoners of war—were sold into slavery. Governor John Winthrop wrote in his journal, "We had now slain and taken in all about seven hundred. We sent fifteen of the boys and two women to Burmuda by Mr. Pierce but he, missing it, carried them to Providence Isle." William Pierce was the captain of the *Desire*, which was built in Marblehead and sailed out of Boston. Providence was a Puritan settlement off the coast of Central America. In February 1638, Captain Pierce returned, bringing "some cotton and tobacco and negroes from thence and salt from Tertugos."[1] The Europeans conquered the Indians to gain their land; they imported Africans to gain their labor.

The story of the voyage of the *Desire* demonstrates the difficulties of recording Afro-American history. We know the name of the ship, where it was built, and the name of its captain, but we do not know the names of the Africans who came as part of its cargo. American histories have been his-

1) John Winthrop, *History of New England from 1610 to 1649*, ed. James Savage (Boston: Little, Brown, 1853), 1:254. Also see Arthur P. Newton, *The Colonizing Activities of the English Puritans* (New Haven: Yale University Press, 1914).

tories of white people, and even these have tended to be of the
well-to-do, the generals, and the winning politicians. To do
Afro-American history, it is necessary to search out new
social historical sources and to reexamine events from the
bottom up. In Massachusetts, unlike the southern colonies,
no legislation was enacted outlawing the education of slaves.
The Puritans had seen the education of Indians as a means of
drawing them away from "savagery" and toward conversion to
Christianity. It would make them "better" Indians. Perhaps
they saw education as making the Africans "better" slaves.
More likely, however, "because of the complex character of
Negro labor . . . it was to the interest of the masters to impart
to the slaves some of the rudiments of learning, for ignorant
workmen . . . were at a disadvantage in the diversified economy of New England."[2]

John Eliot of Roxbury, renowned to the Puritans as "the
apostle to the Indians," became concerned with the education
of Africans late in his life. In 1674, he proposed to the slave
masters within a radius of two or three miles from the Roxbury
meetinghouse to send their slaves to him once a week for
instructions. According to Cotton Mather, Eliot's biographer,
Eliot died before such a class could be established. In 1717,
Mather opened a school for Indians and Negroes, which
lasted at least through that year. Mather's school, with
another established by Nath Pigott in 1728, are the first
organized classes for Africans known to exist in Massachusetts
and probably in all New England.

Organized classes for slave children were rare. The
usual form of education for them was instruction by the master
or members of his family. Seven-year-old Phillis, brought
from Africa to Boston, was purchased by the Wheatley family
in 1761. Her mistress, Susannah Wheatley, instructed her and
trained her to be a domestic in the Wheatley household. Soon
it was discovered that the young African had a talent for
writing poetry; Phillis Wheatley became the first African,
"the first slave and the second woman to publish a book of
poems in the United States." Her talent was exceptional but

---

2) Lorenzo Greene Johnston, *The Negro in Colonial New England* (New York: Atheneum, 1968).

18 her means of education—learning to read and write from her owners—was common. This informal instruction was the first educational system for Afro-Americans in Boston. It depended on a kind or enlightened master or mistress, and it was completely at the whim of the owner.

Although most eighteenth-century Bostonians condoned slavery, at least one, Samuel Sewall, attacked the institution. His booklet, *The Selling of Joseph* (1700), began Boston's long tradition of leadership in the abolition struggle, a movement that influenced some owners to free their slaves. As early as 1720, there are records of free black people living in Boston. Between 1700 and 1776, enough African slaves had gained their freedom through manumission, private agreements with the owner, escape, and, in rare cases, court decisions that a free black community was settled in Boston's North End. White people called their neighborhood the Guinea Coast. Little is known of the education of freed Africans before the 1780s.

The American Revolution was the death knell for slavery in Massachusetts. Some slaves took this opportunity of confusion and disruption among the majority to run away. Because both sides needed manpower, slaves, in return for freedom, fought on both sides. In 1774, Abigail Adams wrote to her husband, John: "There has been in town a conspiracy of the negroes. At present it is kept pretty private. . . . They [drew] up a petition to the Governor, telling him they would fight for him provided he would arm them, and engage to liberate them if he conquered."[3] A number of the black people who had fought on the British side left with the Tory forces when they evacuated Boston, Charleston, South Carolina, and New York. It is estimated that the British took with them somewhere between 10,000 and 15,000 Africans. Most of those black people were taken to Canada and settled in the Maritime Provinces. Between 1780 and 1790, there were several successful court suits challenging slavery as unconstitutional under the state constitution. Slave masters foresaw

---

3) Quoted in Sidney Kaplan, *The Black Presence in the Era of the American Revolution, 1770–1800* (Greenwich, Conn.: Published by the New York Graphic Society in association with Smithsonian Institution Press, 1973).

the demise of slavery, and the number of manumissions
increased. When the first national census was tabulated in
1790, Massachusetts was the only state in the Union to report
no slaves.

The level of optimism in the black community seems to
have been very high in the 1790s. In a generation, one could
have been born free in Africa, been a slave in South Carolina,
been resold in the port of Boston, and now be free. The
leadership of this black community was ready to engage in
increased political and organizing activities. Self-help associ-
ations, such as the African Society of Boston, were formed.
Paul and John Cuffee, black merchants in Westport, Massachusetts, objected to paying taxes since they could not vote.
They were sent to jail, paid their taxes, and later successfully
petitioned the legislature for the right to vote.

In the 1790s, Cato Gardner and the African Society of
Boston urged their members to move to the West End on the
north slope of Beacon Hill. A few, like George Middleton, a
veteran of the War of Independence, moved, but most stayed
in the North End. When the society began to organize a
church, they called a black Baptist preacher, Thomas Paul,
from New Hampshire to organize the congregation. By 1805
he had a sizable number of black people—twenty or thirty
adults—ready to become part of the church and to construct
their own church building. The Free African Society of
Boston persuaded Paul to build the church not where most
black people lived but on the north slope of Beacon Hill.
They built it off Belknap Street—now Joy Street—and called
it the African Meeting House. It was completed in 1806. (It is
still standing and is being restored by the Museum of Afro
American History.) Now black people had an institutional
building. Their previous group activities usually had been
held in white people's institutional buildings or in their own
houses. Now most of those activities moved to this meetinghouse.

Education was one of the main concerns of the black
community, along with the development of independent
institutions (churches and societies), and the plight of the
slave in the southern states. I have found no eighteenth-century statute or regulation in the city of Boston excluding black

20 children from the public schools. But at least by 1798, black parents believed that their children were somehow mistreated, discriminated against, and made to feel unwelcome when they attended Boston schools. References to this treatment are spotty, and most of the discussion in the literature is from forty years later and colored by the abolitionist and anti-segregationist views of the 1840s and 1850s. The parents' response was to request a public school for children of African descent.

In 1798 and again in 1800, black parents—unsuccessfully—petitioned the Boston School Committee to establish a separate public school for their children. Both petitions were denied. The second petition came before a special town meeting. Stanley Schultz calls Boston black parents "one of the first minority groups in any American city to request segregated schools."[4] In 1798, after the first refusal, a private school was organized and located in the home of Primus Hall. Elisha Sylvester, a white man, was the teacher. The school did not last until the end of the year; it closed during a yellow-fever epidemic. In 1802, the school began again in Hall's home, this time with more support from the liberal white community. The teachers were a Mr. Brown and a Mr. Williams, white men from Harvard College; the record is unclear as to whether they were graduates or students.

The school population increased, and in 1808 the school moved to the basement of the two-year-old African Meeting House. At this time the Boston School Committee began to subsidize the school with an annual donation of two hundred dollars. The rest of the school's expenses came from local philanthropy and a tuition of twelve-and-a-half cents per week. In 1808 the school hired its first black teacher, Cyrus Vassall.

The school's second black teacher, Prince Saunders (sometimes spelled Sanders), persuaded Abiel Smith, a white businessman, to write into his will funds for the education of black children in Boston. Smith had already donated a hun-

---

4) Stanley K. Schultz, *The Culture Factory: Boston Public Schools, 1789–1860* (New York: Oxford University Press, 1973), p. 160.

Usually called the African Meeting House this building housed Boston's first church and school for free blacks. The building is currently operated by the Museum of Afro-American History, and is open to the public.

dred dollars to the construction of the meetinghouse on the condition that it be used toward quarters for a "colored school." Smith outlined his proposed bequest to the school committee, and they voted to accept its terms in 1811. Perhaps this knowledge of these forthcoming funds moved the committee to continue its annual two-hundred-dollar subsidy.

In 1817 the first of several Sunday schools was organized for black children and adults. In addition to Bible study, these schools taught reading and writing. The children who attended them were too poor to pay the tuition at the school in the meetinghouse or were unable to attend during the week because they had to work.

By 1821, the meetinghouse school was being called a grammar school and was under the jurisdiction of an annual subcommittee for the African school. The Primary Board investigated primary education among black youngsters and recommended opening two primary schools: one in the North End and one in the West End (Beacon Hill). The West End primary school opened in 1822 in another room in the African Meeting House basement. Another school in the West End and one in the North End were opened, but they lasted for short periods only. With both grammar and primary schools for Afro-Americans, the system was now totally segregated. The primary and grammar school in the African Meeting House basement survived and grew but not without controversy.

The school committee increasingly took control of the day-to-day functioning of the schools, moving into areas that had been controlled by the black parents. In the early 1830s, the parents charged the white master of the school, William Bascom, with incompetence and with "improper familiarities" with female students. The Boston School Committee ruled that the charges were unjustified and would not dismiss him.

For ten years, parents sought a separate building for the African school. In 1834, the school committee voted the funds, and the two-story brick building (which still stands on the corner of Joy Street and Smith) was built next to the African Meeting House. The new schoolhouse was opened in March 1835 and named after Abiel Smith by a vote of the Boston School Committee. Two years after its opening, the Smith School had four teachers instructing three hundred children.

The late 1830s marked the beginning of a new force in the politics of Boston: black and white abolitionists who coalesced both around antislavery demands in the South and civil rights for free black people in the North. In 1832 William Lloyd Garrison organized the New England Anti-Slavery Society at a meeting in the schoolroom of the African Meeting House.

By the 1840s, a generation had gone by since the founding of independent black institutions. The people who had supported separate education inside the black community,

who had wanted all black schools for their children, were old
or had died. Many of the current generation, now starting to
become leaders in the community, had attended these separate schools. One of these people was William C. Nell, who
told why he believed separate education should end. Every
year the Boston School Committee administered a test to des-
ignate the best scholar from each of the grammar schools in
the city. In 1829 Nell, a pupil in the basement school of the
Belknap Street Church, scored highest on the exam administered by a committee member at the Colored School. All the
white scholars were invited to a banquet at Fanueil Hall with
the chairman of the school committee and the mayor, where
they were presented with a medal. But Nell was not allowed to
attend this banquet, and he was given a book, a biography of
Franklin, instead of a medal. Nell decided that he was going
to the banquet. He knew that all the waiters at the banquet
would be black so he persuaded one of them to get him in as a
busboy. In that way he was able to hear all the speeches. The
committeeman who administered the test recognized him and
whispered, "You ought to be here with the other boys." Nell
wanted to say, "If you think so, why have you not taken steps
to bring it about?" But he remained silent. Twenty-six years
later he recalled, "The impression made on my mind, by this
day's experience, deepened into a solemn vow, that, God
helping me, I would do my best to hasten the day when color
of skin would be no barrier to equal school rights."[5]

The abolitionists petitioned the Primary School Board
for the end of separate schools in 1840, 1844, 1845, and 1846.
The 1840 petition was signed by Garrison, Wendell Phillips,
Francis Jackson, Henry W. Williams, and Nell. The 1846
petition was signed by eighty-six black citizens. The first three
were denied without comment. The 1846 petition was denied
with a thirty-eight-page report; two board members issued a
minority report.

In 1844 Nell convinced many black parents to with-

---

5) *Triumph of Equal School Rights in Boston, Proceedings of the Presentation Meeting, December 17, 1885* (Boston, 1856), p. 5. This and eight other documents from the Smith School controversy are reproduced in Leonard W. Levy, *Jim Crow in Boston* (New York: DaCapo, 1974).

draw their children from the Smith School. Over the next few years, attendance at the school dropped slowly. The Boston School Committee's reaction to the agitation was to vote two thousand dollars for repairs to the school in 1849. That same year another petition with over two hundred names was filed against continued separate education. Other parents in favor of keeping the Smith School open organized and became vocal. They petitioned for the status quo and requested that the white master be replaced by a black one. The Boston School Committee agreed and appointed Thomas Paul, Jr., son of the first minister of the African Meeting House. On the first day of school under Paul's direction, the boycotters demonstrated in front of the building, and the police were called to clear the way for the children and teachers to enter.

The antisegregationists now moved their struggle to the courts. Before 1849, Benjamin Roberts had attempted to enroll his daughter, Sarah, in each of the five public schools that stood between their home and the Smith School. When Sarah was denied entrance to all of them, Roberts sued the city under an 1845 statute providing recovery of damages for any child unlawfully denied public school instruction. The abolitionists joined the case in 1849. Charles Sumner represented Sarah, and black attorney Robert Morris acted as cocounsel. The case was was argued before Chief Justice Lemuel Shaw of the Supreme Judicial Court, one of the leading state jurists in the country, whose past opinions had been especially influential. On April 8, 1850, Shaw ruled that Sumner and Roberts had not shown that the Smith School was inferior or that it offered instruction inferior to that in other Boston schools. He saw no problem in having black children attend a separate facility if it were equal. His opinion was the genesis of the separate-but-equal doctrine. Shaw's decision became the definitive one on segregation in the United States. When in *Plessy v. Ferguson,* some thirty years after the Civil War, the issue came to the United States Supreme Court, not around schools but around public transportation, the Supreme Court used and cited Shaw's opinion to justify segregation and Jim Crow legislation.

Black parents were upset, but Nell did not let the momentum drop off. He organized the Equal School Associa-

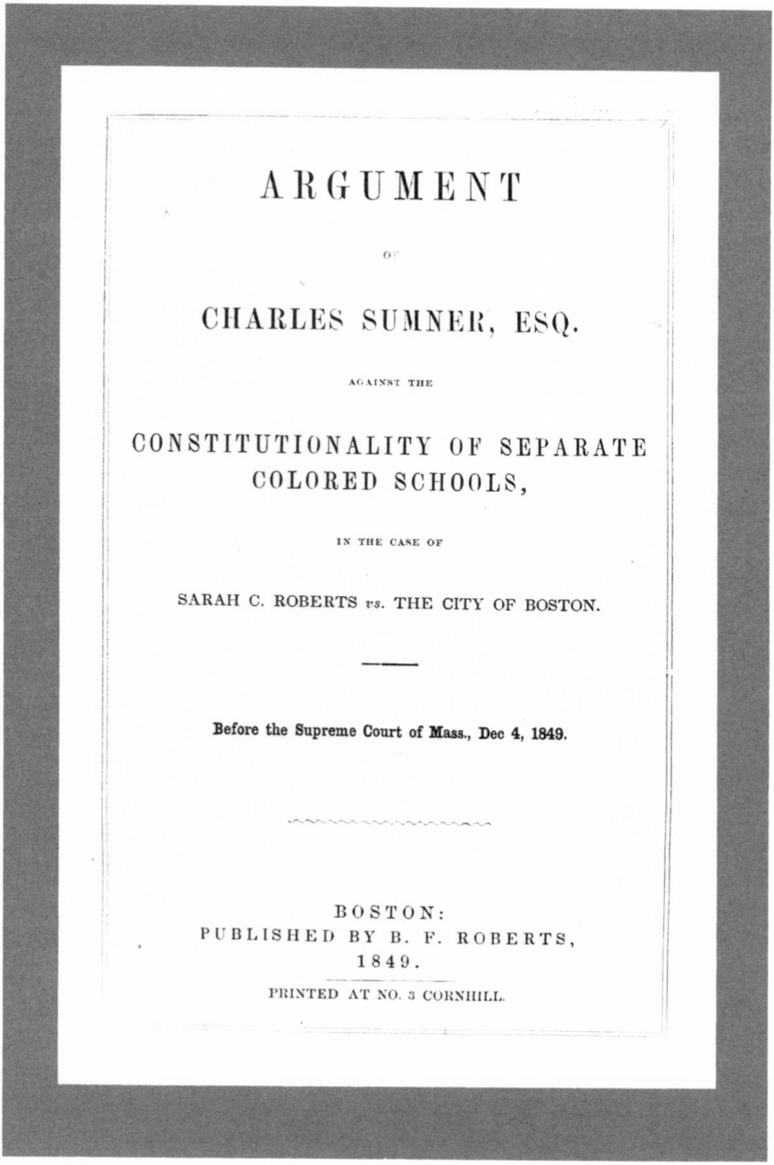

ARGUMENT

OF

CHARLES SUMNER, ESQ.

AGAINST THE

CONSTITUTIONALITY OF SEPARATE COLORED SCHOOLS,

IN THE CASE OF

SARAH C. ROBERTS *vs.* THE CITY OF BOSTON.

Before the Supreme Court of Mass., Dec 4, 1849.

BOSTON:
PUBLISHED BY B. F. ROBERTS,
1849.

PRINTED AT NO. 3 CORNHILL.

While the arguments in the Sarah Roberts case were not successful in ending Boston's legal segregation of its schools, the case played an important role in building public sentiment against segregation so that within six years the state legislature would enact its legal demise.

tion of Boston, which attempted to bring the issue of segregated public education before the Massachusetts legislature. The 1850s in Boston were turbulent times. The abolitionists were gaining more and more electoral power. At the same time, the movement in the city against foreigners was coming to a head, and a number of nativist (anti-immigrant) groups were organized in Massachusetts. Among these was the Know-Nothing party, which was organized both to keep foreigners out of the country and to force those that were in the country to act in "the proper" way. Proper meant more like Yankee Protestants. Interestingly the Know-Nothing party contained a number of abolitionists who were antislavery and anti-Catholic. Of course, most black people at this time had been born in the United States, and they were Protestant. Both abolitionists and Know-Nothings were running for city and state office and, especially after 1853, winning. Yet between 1850 and 1853 the attitude of the school committee remained unchanged. In 1852 a black couple who lived in East Boston petitioned the committee to allow their son and daughter to attend the grammar school in East Boston. The committee refused, but it provided ferry money so the children could attend the Smith School. In 1854, as political conditions changed, a student of black, white, and Indian descent enrolled in a white school. When the case came before the school committee, it ruled that the child could stay in the white school. Moreover a committee that reviewed the case recommended to the school committee that segregation be ended in Boston's schools.

Nell and the Equal School Association pushed their cause in the halls of the state house. A bill to end segregation in public schools failed in 1851, but a similar measure was passed by the legislators in 1855 and was signed by the governor in April. It outlawed segregation in the state's public schools, although the only segregated system by now was in Boston. Thus the combination of rising anti-slavery sentiment, the growing strength of the abolitionists, the support of Know-Nothing politicians, and the determination of many black parents to end segregated education, brought a dramatic, if short-lived, change to Boston's schools.

On September 3, 1855, black students accompanied by

their mothers enrolled in the previously all-white schools nearest to their homes. The opening day and subsequent ones were peaceful. Later that year Nell said, "And since the 3rd of September to the present time, the sun, moon and stars are regular in their courses! No orb has proved so eccentric as to shoot madly from its sphere in consequence, and the State House on Beacon, and old Faneuil Hall, remain as firm on their bases as ever."[6] The student bodies remained desegregated in Boston for another twenty years. However, no black teachers from the Smith School were hired, and black teachers did not reenter the Boston system until the 1890s. After the Civil War, the black population of Boston increased considerably—by 400 percent between 1865 and 1875—and the north slope, which had been integrated, became predominately black. Schools like the Phillips School that were integrated in 1855 were predominately black in 1880. A study issued that year by the United States commissioner on education noted that the Phillips school (on the corner of Pinckney and Anderson Streets) was regularly called the "Colored School." This was the beginning of Boston's *de facto* segregation.

In the 1890s the black middle class cited a desire for better schools as one of their reasons for moving to Cambridge, the South End, and Roxbury. The changing housing development and the influx of newer immigrants onto the north slope forced the black working class and poor to move to Lower Roxbury and two neighborhoods in the South End. For a time a semblance of desegregation was regained due to the integration of these neighborhoods. Throughout the twentieth century, however, as Boston's black population continued to grow, a pattern of resegregation developed. After World War II, the school committee more actively instituted *de jure* segregation, giving rise to a decade and a half of civil rights protests beginning in the early 1960s. Boston schools had come full circle in relation to equal opportunity for black children.

---

6) Ibid, p. 9.

CHAPTER 3

Reform, Immigration, and Bureaucracy, 1820–1870

JAMES W. FRASER

Horace Mann, Secretary of the Massachusetts Board of Education from 1837 to 1848, dominated much of the thinking about schooling, both in Boston and throughout the nation, in the first half of the nineteenth century.

The reformers of the Revolutionary era who reorganized Boston's schools, founded the Boston School Committee, in 1789, and went on—in the face of considerable opposition—to open the primary school system in 1820 never dreamed of the changes to these schools and to their city that the next four decades would bring. Between 1820 and 1860, the population of Boston jumped from 43,000 to 178,000. Boston in these years changed from a large town that retained the colonial sense of compactness and interdependence to a modern city with all of the problems of class conflict, anonymity, and confusion. During these years, the growth in school enrollment was phenomenal. The combined primary and grammar school enrollment for 1820 was 4,500; before 1860, the number had passed 25,000. Even more difficult for the city and the schools, what had been a relatively homogeneous town for over a century became one of the major centers for the new immigrants coming to the United States from Europe, especially from Ireland. In 1820 the foreign-born population of Boston had been 12 percent; by 1860 it was 53 percent.

During these years, the idealogy of the proper role of schools in a democratic society was being challenged. The changes were due in part to immigration and the extraordinary internal growth of the population. But more was going on. The primary educational institutions of colonial America—the family and the church—were both losing prestige. Urbanization and industrialization ended the dominant role of the family as the economic and apprenticeship center. Where rural sons and daughters had learned their trades from their farmer parents, the children of factory workers could not follow the family-oriented pattern. The variety and diversity that institutional religion was adopting in the new United States and the final separation of the Congregational church from the commonwealth of Massachusetts in 1833 meant that no church could set the moral tone for a community. Into this void the public school, which in colonial society had been a rather marginal institution to teach certain skills, moved with new prominence. Stanley Schultz states the new role well: "The public school was to be a classroom, a family room, a church house—all

30 things to all children."[1] Not only were the schools to continue their role of teaching reading, writing, and arithmetic, they were to make citizens for the new republic. Nowhere was this new responsibility taken more seriously than in the old city of Boston.

The so-called common school revival has often been associated with Horace Mann's tenure as secretary of the Massachusetts Board of Education from 1837 to 1848. Although many throughout New England and on the western frontier played roles similar to Mann's, Mann gave voice to the movement better than any of the others. And certainly in his home town of Boston, Horace Mann was the dominant symbol of the new-found faith in the importance of the public schools. "Without undervaluing any other human agency," he wrote,

> it may be safely affirmed that the Common School, improved and energized, as it can easily be, may become the most effective and benignant of all the forces of civilization . . . when its faculties shall be fully developed, when it shall be trained to wield its mighty energies for the protection of society against the giant vices which now invade and torment it;— against intemperance, avarice, war, slavery, bigotry, the woes of want and the wickedness of waste;—then there will not be a height to which these enemies of the race can escape, which it will not scale nor a Titan among them all, whom it will not slay.[2]

That is "true faith" and that is what Horace Mann argued that the school would do. Mann was born in Franklin, Massachusetts, in 1796 and was educated rather briefly in the town schools; he seems to have attended for a year or two when a schoolmaster was in town. He attended Brown University,

---

1) Stanley K. Schultz, *The Culture Factory: Boston Public Schools, 1789–1860.* (New York: Oxford University Press, 1973), p. 69. Schultz's excellent study of the early history of the Boston schools has been an invaluable asset in the development of this essay.

2) Horace Mann, "Twelfth Annual Report" (1848) in Lawrence A. Cremin, ed., *The Republic and the School: Horace Mann on the Education of Free Men* (New York: Teachers College Press, 1957), p. 80.

became a lawyer, and for ten years (1826–1837) was a member of the Massachusetts legislature and then, when an aspiring candidate for governor, chose instead in 1837 to become the first secretary of the newly established Massachusetts Board of Education, an office with virtually no power except to compile statistics on the schools. He used the position to express his faith that the school could become society's most important institution and unite the American people. "It may be an easy thing to make a Republic," Mann wrote in one of his reports, "but it's a very laborious thing to make Republicans."[3] The role of the school, Mann thought, was to take on that task of making future citizens into loyal participants in the emerging nation. A new institution was needed, he argued, because the church, which had done that in the past, could no longer function in that way. Most of the colonial states had had an established church. The Congregational Church (both Unitarian and Trinitarian) was the official state church in Massachusetts until 1833; their ministers were paid by the commonwealth and were seen as civil servants. But even before the church was disestablished, a variety of churches were offering healthy competition. The church would not unite the society any longer so something new had to come in and teach a common core of faith. For Horace Mann the public school was the institution. All people in the society would move through the school. When Mann talked about a common school, he did not mean a school for the common people; he meant a school that would be common to all the people—the upper class, the working class, and the middle class. All would have a common experience, which would build a united society in America.

Mann argued that it was important for the public school to have ample public support. He wrote again and again that private money was not for any one generation; it was a trust. Therefore taxation for schools was appropriate because it was for the benefit of the whole society. In case some people were not convinced by Mann's altruistic rhetoric about public responsibility, he also wrote to the rich:

---

3) Ibid., p. 92.

32   Finally, in regard to those who possess the largest shares in the stock of worldly goods, could there, in your opinion, be any police so vigilant and effective, for the protection of all the rights of person, property and character, as such a sound and comprehensive education and training, as our system of Common Schools could be made to impart; and would not the payment of sufficient tax to make such education and training universal, be the cheapest means of self-protection and insurance![4]

This argument that schools are cheaper than prisons is still used.

Finally Mann argued that the schools should not only be supported publicly, they should be controlled publicly. Every town should have an elected board of education to represent the people directly in controlling the schools. As he wrote in his charge to the board, "In the contemplation of the law, the school committees are sentinels stationed at the door of every schoolhouse in the State, to see that no teacher ever crosses its threshold, who is not clothed, from the crown of his head to the sole of his foot, in garments of virtue."[5]

Mann, along with Boston politicians like Samuel Gridley Howe and George Emerson, proposed numerous changes in Boston's school ways. The numerical expansion of the system alone would have demanded this, but other forces were also at work. Commentators on the Boston scene regularly alternated between praise for the Boston system as the "richest Jewel in New England's crown" and the memory of Boston students like Edward Everett Hale that "it was on the monotony of school life that my dislike was founded."[6] Parents and neighborhood leaders also struggled with school reformers over the degree of local versus centralized control the schools

---

4) Horace Mann, "Fifth Report" (1841), in Cremin, *Republic and the School,* p. 53.

5) Horace Mann, "Fourth Report" (1840), in Cremin, *Republic and the School,* p. 52.

6) *Boston School Reports* (Boston, 1846), p. 160, cited by Schultz, *Culture Factory,* p. 108. Edward Everett Hale, *A New England Boyhood* (1893; reprinted , Boston, 1964), p. 26, cited in Schultz, *Culture Factory,* p. 108.

should receive. The issue of neighborhood schools was further complicated by much confusion on the issue of whether boys and girls should go to school separately or together, for sexual segregation often required longer commutes between home and school buildings for half of the student population.

In the spring of 1843 Mann traveled to Europe to observe schools there. He was especially attracted by the order of the Prussian system and the apparent happiness of the students. In his report for 1843, he noted that in Prussia "I heard no child ridiculed, sneered at, or scolded for making a mistake."[7] The comparison with Boston was obvious and angered many of the schoolmasters, both because they felt demeaned and because some feared the importation of the far more hierarchical, and less democratic, Prussian educational arrangements.

An immediate result of Mann's Prussian experience for Boston was the development of the first graded school in the nation. In response to the Mann report, Howe and Emerson, both then school committee members, suggested several changes in the schools, including written examinations, more careful moral training, and the organization of the classes by groups of similar ability. The advantages would be not only more careful supervision and instruction but a much higher level of uniformity throughout the city.

In the fall of 1847, the Quincy School opened under the leadership of John D. Philbrick, later to be superintendent in Boston, as an experimental graded school. The children were divided into twelve separate classrooms, each with their own teacher, and classified so that they could move systematically through the levels. The degree of control and uniformity seemed to please everyone involved and within fifteen years the experiment had spread to every primary and grammar school in Boston. By the end of the century, the graded school would become the American way of schooling in all areas with enough students to allow for such arrangements.

As the schools became more and more tightly administered, the curriculum also changed. The *New England Primer*,

---

7) Horace Mann, "Seventh Report" (1843), in Cremin, *Republic and the School*, p. 55.

The Quincy School, the first school in the nation to divide students according to grade level, opened on Tyler Street in 1847 as a symbol of the reforms of Horace Mann's era.

with its focus on teaching the child to "fear God and honor the King," would no longer do. A new author was emerging to dominate American school texts—at least those in use east of the Alleghenies—for the next half-century. In 1783 Noah Webster, perhaps most famous for his dictionary, had published the first part of his *Grammatical Institute of the English Language*, designed explicitly to be a new curriculum for the nation's schools. After a somewhat slow start, the Webster curriculum caught on. By the turn of the century sales were at 200,000 copies per year, and as late as the 1880s they remained at over a million.[8] Through the Webster series, which consisted of a reader, a speller, and a grammar text, the child would learn reading and writing and at the same time would be instructed in the civic virtues, which Webster, like Mann

---

8) Noah Webster, *The American Spelling Book, Containing the Rudiments of the English Language for the Use of Schools in the United States* (1831; reprinted, New York: Teachers College Press, 1958), p. iii. While the Webster series remained the most popular school text throughout the nineteenth century on the East Coast, it was replaced throughout most of the West by the even more well-known *McGuffey Readers*.

A
Grammatical Inſtitute,

OF THE

ENGLISH LANGUAGE,

COMPRISING,

An eaſy, conciſe, and ſyſtematic Method of

EDUCATION,

Deſigned for the Uſe of *Engliſh* Schools

IN *AMERICA.*

IN THREE PARTS.

PART II.

CONTAINING,

A plain and comprehenſive Grammar, grounded on the true Principles and Idioms of the Language; with an analytical Diſſertation, in which the various Uſes of the Auxiliary Signs are unfolded and explained: And an Eſſay towards inveſtigating the Rules of Engliſh Verſe.

BY NOAH WEBSTER, Jun. Eſq.

Uſus eſt Norma Loquendi.   CICERO.

HARTFORD:

PRINTED BY HUDSON & GOODWIN, FOR THE AUTHOR, M,DCC,LXXXIV.

Under Protection of the Statute.

Noah Webster's famous textbook designed for the schools of the new nation was the basic text in antebellum Boston.

36 and his colleagues, believed to be essential for republican citizens.

Webster's title for his new series—*An American Selection of Lessons in Reading and Speaking Calculated to Improve the Minds and Refine the Taste of Youth and Also to Instruct Them in Geography and Politics of the United States in Which Prefix Rules in Elocution and Directions for Expressing the Principal Patterns of the Mind*—stated his goals. First, the lessons were designed to improve the mind and refine the taste, and thereby build moral people. The second goal was to teach the geography, history, and politics of the United States. And it was not an unbiased view of any of those. The new nation was portrayed as the promised land. And finally, the program was to teach reading and writing. People had been learning to read and write a long time before Webster or Mann came along, and the school might teach these things as well as its predecessors, but the primary goal of this new institution was to build citizenship. As Webster put his motto on the title page of his first book, "Begin with the infant in the cradle, let the first word from his lips be Washington."

Through all of his many public pronouncements on education, Horace Mann consistently kept the focus on the building of citizens for the future. But Mann, like so many other reformers, was often looking to the past as his model. In some ways it was almost as if he were trying to build citizens for the town of Franklin, Massachusetts, where he had grown. But many groups in Boston had never had much role in towns like Franklin. First of all were the Roman Catholic immigrants. The schools were clearly a Protestant venture. They were to replace one established Protestant church by teaching a common core, as Mann stated the faith: "In this age of the world, it seems to me that no student of history, or observer of mankind, can be hostile to the precepts and doctrines of the Christian religion. . . . The Bible is the acknowledged expositor of Christianity. In strictness, Christianity has no other authoritative expounder. The Bible is in our Common Schools, by common consent."[9] The schools would be open

---

9) Horace Mann, "Twelfth Report" (1848) in Cremin, *Republic and the School*, pp. 102, 105.

to Methodists and Baptists, as well as to Congregationalists and Unitarians, according to Mann, but he never mentioned Roman Catholics, and there were increasing numbers of them in Massachusetts. The fact that Roman Catholics did not believe that Christianity had no other authoritative expounder than the Bible was simply ignored. Second, Mann's schools almost completely ignored nonwhites. There had not been many nonwhites in Franklin, Massachusetts. But in Boston and in other parts of Massachusetts there were blacks and native Americans. The schools were set up virtually as if they did not exist. Finally, the schools ignored anyone who was too poor to have the leisure to attend them. For many of the children of poor families, there was no time for school; the income from their work in factories was too badly needed at home. Mann simply ignored that reality. Recent studies have shown that poor people, contrary to what Horace Mann would have expected, often voted against school taxes.[10] Even though the tax for them was rather minimal, there was no advantage to paying it because they were excluded from the benefits. Here indeed is a paradox: the schools were being set up in part to control and assimilate immigrants and poor people, but in practice they often excluded them.

That paradox, like all of the other issues faced by Boston's school leaders, was compounded far beyond their earlier imagining by a new development in the mid-1840s: Irish immigration. It was one thing to deal with a city whose population was growing rapidly from high birthrate and the immigration from the countryside of Yankee farmers. It was quite another to deal with a population growing yet faster because new settlers were coming, settlers who shared none of the nationalistic feelings, cultural assumptions, or religion of those who were meeting them.

Boston had long received immigrants from Europe who were seeking political asylum or simply a better chance, but the numbers remained small, and most who arrived in the port moved west. During no year prior to 1840 did the number

---

10) See for example Michael B. Katz, *The Irony of Early School Reform* (Boston: Beacon Press, 1968).

of immigrants from all sources reach 4,000. By 1849 the figure was 29,000, with most of the increase coming directly or indirectly from Ireland.[11] There were several factors unique to the arrival of the Boston Irish. Most significantly, they were not coming to something; they were fleeing for their lives from Ireland. The Irish economy had been dismal for decades, but the potato famine of 1846–1851 and the refusal of British landlords to make other foods available led to the deaths of a million Irish people, 25 percent of the total population. Anyone who could, escaped, and the cheapest rates were to Boston. Those who arrived came out of desperation; they had no remaining funds, few industrial skills, and a deep hatred of all things British, an attitude that would soon be transferred to the British ways of Yankee Boston, especially because the new arrivals were met with the open hostility of an increasing nativist, anti-Catholic population.

By 1860 there were as many immigrants who called themselves Irish as there were Yankees and the stage was set for the major battles that would dominate Boston's economy and politics—and therefore schools—for the next century. While other American cities received a variety of immigrants and western cities received their European and American settlers at the same time, Boston was unique. Here a long-established native population received immigrants of one ethnic group, which became cohesive in its own ways. Trouble was inevitable.

As has so often happened in American history, the poor were blamed for all of the problems they faced. The Irish were seen as drunks; they were the ones arrested; they were the ones on the poor rolls. As early as the 1820s, there had been anti-Catholic riots in Boston, and these grew in number and intensity as the Catholic population grew. Attacks on Irish people and Irish property attested to the depth of the animosity.

While working-class native Protestants might engage in riots and support nativist societies out of fear of new competitors for scarce New England jobs, Boston's elite found

---

11) Oscar Handlin, *Boston's Immigrants, 1790–1880* (Cambridge, Mass.: Harvard University Press, 1941; reprinted New York: Atheneum, 1976), pp. 51-52.

other methods to deal with their fears. There was tremendous fear, openly stated in school committee reports, year after year, of class and ethnic consciousness and class and religious warfare. Mayor Josiah Quincy reminded the city that the working class must be taught to "look upon the distinctions of society without envy." The schools, which had already taken on the task of assimilation among different native groups, must redouble their efforts with these new arrivals who needed yet more assimilation, especially since their religion did not fit into the general Protestant consensus that dominated Boston society and schools. Quincy went on, "All children must be taught to respect and revere law and order."[12] And the school committee took up the challenge to "save society not with the cannon and the rifle, but with the spelling book, the grammar, and the Bible."[13] They were confident they could accomplish the task.

In 1848, in their annual report to the city of Boston, the school committee members wrote, "We shall have little to fear from the much talked of dangers of immigration, if the rising generation of immigrants can thus be brought practically to understand . . . that the State will take equal care of them, as of the children of the soil."[14] Schools were the solution. They would being everyone together, assimilate everyone, and make every Irish Catholic a good Yankee. The problem of school attendance became acute. The schools were set to do their assigned task, but the children were not necessarily going to the schools and there were not enough places for them all. As early as the 1820s, Massachusetts law required each child to work, furnish explicit proof of why he should not go to school, or register for the public school. But having registered, it was virtually impossible to make a child attend the school. And while significant numbers of poor immigrant children were sent to the workhouse for being "incorrigibly stubborn" or "habitually truant," there was no effective com-

---

12) Schultz, p. 256.

13) Quoted in Schultz, *Culture Factory*, p. 260, from a speech by Edward Everett Hale.

14) *Report of the Annual Examination of the Public Schools of the City of Boston* (Boston, 1848), p. 22, cited by Schultz, *Culture Factory*, p. 278.

pulsory education law. By the 1850s a consensus was emerging that the situation had to change if the school was to accomplish its important role of assimilation. In 1850, the Massachusetts state legislature, under strong pressure from the Boston School Committee, passed a law authorizing the towns and cities to make any needed provisions for habitual and unemployed truants and to establish penalties for parents who profited from their "wretched gains or dishonest pursuits." Objections had been raised by some of the legislators that this legislation threatened the parents' right over the child. But they were told that such influences are not properly exerted by the parents, especially among the poorer classes. In other words, parents had control over their children as long as they did with them what the state thought would be correct. Boston responded promptly to this new law and hired the first full-time truant officer in America.

In 1852 the legislature went further—again at the prompting of the Boston School Committee—by specifically requiring every child between the ages of eight and fourteen to attend public school for at least three consecutive months of the year. Parents who kept their children from attending school were subject to a fine. This was very limited compulsory education by today's standards, but by 1852 the pattern was set. After that, it was simply a matter of expanding the age brackets and the number of days per year that children had to attend.

During the same years that schooling was becoming compulsory in Massachusetts, the school system was being bureaucratized and professionalized. Before 1850 Boston's schools did not have much of a bureaucracy, and there were no professional administrators—only teachers and lay school committee members. In 1850 there was no school employee above the level of teacher. There were visiting committees, subcommittees of the Boston School Committee, which went around to each school four or five times each year to inspect. If they liked what they saw, the teacher's contract was renewed; if they did not, the teacher was terminated. Teachers reported with some regularity to the school committee, but there were no officers in charge of checking up on them, helping them, or supervising them. Relatively few records were kept, so there was no need for much paperwork.

In 1845 a Boston School Committee report—inspired by Mann and his allies—pointed to a need for a superintendent of public schools to provide "permanence, personal responsibility, continued and systematic labor."[15] They needed one person for whom the schools would be a full-time job. Those who wrote the report believed that the many part-time members of the school committee could not keep up with the kind of supervision they were doing. Opponents raised the argument that the schools were to be public and publicly controlled, and control ought therefore to rest with part-time people, average citizens. Citizen control, it was said, would be reduced by having a paid bureaucracy. The reformers countered, "In recent years citizens had often registered complaints about some individuals using their position on the School Committee as a stepping-stone to political advancement or personal profit."[16] In 1851 a joint committee of the school committee and the city council agreed that the appointment of a superintendent "would add greatly to their [the schools'] efficiency and usefulness, and ought not longer to be delayed."[17] The council appropriated $2,500 for a salary, and Nathan Bishop was hired from a similar position in Providence, Rhode Island. Once this full-time administration was launched the number of administrators and the attendant bureaucracy grew steadily. In 1866 the masters of the grammar schools—the senior teachers of the grammar schools—were appointed to be the principals of all the primary schools in their districts. Boston still operated on the two-level system: grammar schools for children eight to fourteen, and primary schools to teach basic reading to children between four and eight. Several primary schools would feed into a grammar school. But, until this time, there was no structural link between the two. Now the head teacher of the grammar school, the master, would supervise the work of the primary

---

15) *Boston School Reports* (Boston, 1845), pp. 33-34, cited by Schultz, *Culture Factory*, p. 145.

16) Ibid., p. 34, cited by Schultz, *Culture Factory*, p. 146.

17) City of Boston. Report on Superintendent of Public Schools (March 1851), in *Boston City Documents*, 1851, doc. 16, cited by Schultz, *Culture Factory*, p. 151.

school teachers. In 1875 the Board of Supervisors was created; it consisted of six people to supervise the masters and work with the superintendent. And in the ten years between 1866 and 1876, sixty-four special instructors were added to the school system's rolls, including fourteen truant officers. By 1875, the bureaucracy was functioning fully. Its growth would be challenged at times, but never halted. By 1876 most of the fixtures of the modern school system were in place.

The development of this bureaucratic system was not unrelated to the other developments in Boston's schools. Bureaucracies became popular in many parts of American life after the civil war, particularly in industry, but bureaucracy in public education fit well with other reforms going on, and it served similar purposes. It may have worked to make educational systems more efficient and uniform. But the development of a professional bureaucracy also played an important role in removing control of and access to the decision making process from the majority of citizens. Some objected, but not too many. The older Bostonians, who a half-century earlier would never have agreed to giving up some of their democratic rights in the field of education, were becoming increasingly distrustful of some forms of democracy. Democracy, after all, was one thing when they were the vast majority, but as newer immigrants came to make up more and more of the population, it became increasingly important to these Yankees to have control of some of the traditional institutions vested elsewhere. A bureaucratized school system—led of course by well educated professionals—could be one more means of accomplishing the same mixture of ends that most of the other late-nineteenth century school reforms served.

CHAPTER 4

Boston Catholics and the School Question, 1825–1907

JAMES W.
SANDERS*

The ruins of the Ursuline Convent in Charlestown.

*This chapter contains material from a forthcoming book to be published by Oxford University Press. The author gratefully acknowledges support for research from the National Endowment for the Humanities, the City University of New York Faculty Research Award program, and the Center for the Study of American Catholicism, University of Notre Dame.

On the night of August 11, 1834, after several days of threatening demonstrations, an angry mob destroyed the Ursuline convent and boarding school in Charlestown, just outside Boston. They pillaged the entire twenty-four-acre establishment, put to flight the women and children occupants, and even desecrated the tombs in a fruitless search for skeletons of the nuns' illegitimate infants. The incident horrified and appalled right-minded people of all persuasions and precipitated anguished reflection on both the social and moral conditions that caused the outrage and possible preventative measures for the future. Not everyone arrived at the same conclusions.

Horace Mann considered the convent burning a horrible outrage. He had, at the moment, ample time to brood on the event. After his wife's death two years before, Mann had lapsed into despondency, almost abandoning a promising career as a young lawyer, member of the state legislature, and champion of temperance and other reforms. He lived, literally, in his Boston law office and seemed in every respect a man disposed to suicide were it not for a deeply ingrained Yankee morality and a certain morbid conviction that he was born to suffer. His friends, having tried in vain to shake his lethargy and return him to public life, now seized upon the Charlestown affair to effect their purpose. They proposed him as counsel for a special mayoral committee charged with investigating the burning. Mann's outrage compelled him to accept, and he reentered a career that eventually led to his role as father of the American public school.

Later events made the intimate connection between this outbreak of anti-Catholicism in Boston and the choice of a new career as advocate of public education clear and compelling to Mann. Indeed as he weighed the decision to abandon politics for the position as Massachusetts' first state superintendent of schools in 1837, a serious anti-Irish riot broke out on Broad Street in Boston. Mann was again shocked by the growing disrespect for order in Boston and the disruptive social forces that seemed to be tearing the city apart by destroying the old cohesion in the face of urbanization, industrialization, and immigration. The threat of anarchy and violence seemed imminent. The traditional guardians of order, family and church, stood powerless to prevent the catastrophe. What better remedy, concluded Mann, than the common school, where children of all creeds, ethnic origins, and economic circumstance could intermingle on common ground and form the nucleus of a new, more harmonious society? Thus the Charlestown convent and the Broad Street riot helped lead Mann directly into his role as champion of the common school crusade.

The convent burning led Benedict Fenwick, the second Catholic bishop of Boston, to quite different conclusions and a diametrically opposed course of action. Fenwick had personally chosen the property in Charlestown for the Ursuline convent and school, supervised every detail of its building, and done most of the landscaping himself. He went there weekly to examine the students or attend their performances or minister to the nuns' spiritual needs. Mount Benedict, as the nuns had named it in his honor, was not just another convent, not just another school. Other than a class for girls taught by the Sisters of Charity in the cathedral basement, it was the only Catholic school in New England. It was also the most expensive and best-developed piece of Catholic property. The Ursuline nuns who taught there and supervised the some sixty boarders represented the best in French culture and attracted many Protestant girls from the first families of Boston and New England.

The convent's total destruction understandably shocked Bishop Fenwick. Though at first buoyed by the cries of outrage from Boston's leading citizens, his hopes for good coming out of evil evaporated and then turned to cynical despair in the chilling aftermath. Every one of the instigators, despite their known participation, was acquitted. Petitions to indemnify the convent, based on the known fact that Charlestown authorities had provided no protection despite ample warning, were refused by the state legislature. And as a small but fitting capstone to the injustice, two months later, the Charlestown tax collector insisted on levying the annual assessment.

In the first expression of emotion recorded in his diary since taking office in 1825, Fenwick lamented: "No law or justice to be expected in this land where Catholics are constantly

46 calumniated and the strongest prejudices exist against them. Shame!!"[1] The conviction that justice for Catholics could not be expected in New England set him unalterably on a separatist course, so much so, in fact, that in the future establishment of Catholic schools he forbade the admission of Protants. On one occasion he boasted, "I shall erect a College into which no Protestant shall ever set foot."[2] Thus the same incident that led Horace Mann to attempt using the schools to remake society led Benedict Fenwick to attempt to create a separate school system and society.

Probably in no other American city did Catholics have more provocation to do so. Nowhere was there a longer or deeper tradition of anti-Catholicism. Until 1780, 150 years after its founding, Massachusetts denied freedom of worship to Catholics. Not until 1820 could Catholics hold public office. Until 1833 tax monies went to the support of Protestant churches. Until 1862 the public schools officially taught Protestantism. And until 1883 Catholics in city prisons, orphanages, and the like attended compulsory Protestant religious services. As late as 1905 church spokesmen fought for legislation to safeguard the religious beliefs of Catholic orphans.

These restrictions represented merely the legal tip of a much deeper antagonism that hearkened back to the Reformation and more immediately into the exclusionary Puritan theology. Nor did the gradual removal of legal inequities eradicate the pervasive hostility to Catholicism in Massachusetts. That process crept much more slowly. In Boston, in fact, antagonisms seemed to increase even as legal restrictions lifted. This was due to the profound social, economic, and political changes that attended the influx of Catholics through the nineteenth century.

As late as 1820 Boston could be described as "singularly homogeneous, . . . eminently English in its character and appearance, and probably no town of its size in England had a

---

1) Memorandum, December 12, 1834, Boston Archdiocesan Archives.

2) Fenwick to Rev. George Fenwick, November 29, 1838, Fordham University Archives, 202-M-7.

population of such unmixed English descent."[3] In 1820 the
single Catholic parish founded in 1788 and elevated to cathedral status in 1808, had only 2,000 parishioners in a city of
over 43,000 people. Catholics were still a novelty, and many
Bostonians had grown to adulthood without ever having seen
a Catholic priest. The one they saw most now, the French
priest and bishop, Jean Cheverus (1808–1823), projected a
genuinely learned, gentle humanity. His urbane yet simple
mode of life blended well into the Boston scene, and he
basked in the positive afterglow of his mother country's participation in the American Revolution.

But most of Cheverus's flock was Irish, and by the time
Benedict Fenwick (1825–1846) took over, the storm cloud of
large-scale Irish immigration had crossed the horizon. By
1825 the Catholic population of Boston reached a noticeable
8.6 percent of the total. Although the more liberal Unitarians
and respectable Episcopalians maintained outward equilib-
rium, the evangelical sects and the orthodox Calvinists took
alarm. By the late 1820s, Boston's religious press was spewing
out reams of anti-Catholic vituperation, to which the belli-
cose Fenwick replied with equal stridency. The Charlestown
convent burning of 1834 climaxed that first outbreak of
Boston nativism, but it did not begin or end it. The anti-Irish
riots that started in 1823 continued sporadically through the
1830s, while home missionary societies formed ranks to con-
vert the Catholics from idolatry.

Beneath the occasional violence and the verbal broad-
sides laden with conflicting theologies and doctrinal dispute
lay the fundamental social fear that Irish Catholics were
invading Boston. By Fenwick's death in 1846, the Catholic
proportion of the city had risen to 26 percent, an alarming
figure for many Protestants.

But for brahmin Boston the worst had yet to come. The
potato famine of the late 1840s brought thousands of Irish
Catholic peasants to Boston. Their poverty placed a crushing
financial burden on the city's welfare agencies, and their des-

---

3) Edmund Quincy, *The Life of Josiah Quincy of Massachusetts* (Boston: Ticknor
and Fields, 1867), p. 396.

48   peration for jobs put them in conflict with native labor. More appalling still, at the urging of the Irish Catholic press and with the help of eager politicians, they began to seek citizenship and reach for the ballot. Thus by the early 1850s, when the Catholic population had reached at least 40 percent of the total, the old religious antagonisms had been greatly compounded and enflamed by the ominous consequences of immigration. The result was a second great awakening of nativism in Boston—the Know-Nothing movement, which swept into control of the city and state in the mid-1850s and included such legislation as mandatory reading of the Protestant Bible in public school and such absurdities as a Nunnery Committee of the state legislature to inspect convents.

Little wonder, then, that the separatist sentiment grew among Catholic Bostonians. As their organ, the *Pilot*, put it in 1839: "It is truly marvelous and somewhat amusing to hear the most exclusive and illiberal people on the face of the earth complain that foreigners do not mingle and unite with them. As well might the trapper find fault with the game who will not run into his guns. Do not the Irish know that the embrace of this people is destruction, and that they can mingle with them on no other condition but that of abject servitude? Have they not had abundant evidence that the Yankees only love foreigners as the hunter loves the deer?"[4]

Given such sentiments, one would expect to find Bishop Fenwick's determination to develop a separate institutional system for Boston Catholics carried out in fullest detail. Yet as regards parochial elementary schools, such was not the case. When Fenwick came to Boston, the single Catholic school enrolled 1.4 percent of the combined public school–Catholic school student population in the city. At his death in 1846, Catholic schools accounted for 2.8 percent, a very modest gain over 1825 but in fact an actual loss of ground since the city was now over a quarter Catholic. Chart 1 tells the story. The two best available statistical indicators of Catholic commitment to parochial schooling—the percentage of parishes with schools of their own and the relative proportion of children in Catholic schools—both indicate an extremely

---

4) *Pilot*, June 22, 1839.

modest growth after 1825. By 1907 fewer than half the Catholic parishes in Boston had parochial schools, and these educated only 15.7 percent of the school children in a city almost
half Catholic. Even in parishes with schools, the majority of
Catholic children attended public school. The statistics for
every earlier year are even less favorable. Taken together, the
figures suggest a kind of collective ambivalence in Boston
Catholicism's approach to parochial education.

Chart 1
BOSTON

Year	Parishes	Schools	% Parishes with Schools	Catholic Elementary School Enrollment	Public Elementary School Enrollment	% in Catholic Schools	Boston Population	% Catholic Population of Boston
1820							43,298	
1825	1	1	100	60	4,156	1.4		8.6
1830							61,392	
1846	7	2	29	500	17,110	2.8		26.2
1850							136,881	
1859	10	2	20	900	25,315	3.6		45
1860							177,841	
1866	12	5	42	3,345	27,723	10.7		45
1870							250,526	
1880	27	10	37	5,787	50,412	10.3	362,839	45
1890	33	14	42	8,531	58,080	12.8	448,477	45
1900	44	19	43	12,401	72,672	14.6	560,892	45
1907	53	24	45	16,826	90,086	15.7		45

The answer to this middle-of-the-road result appears to
lie in a variety of interrelated factors, which, taken together,
account for a lackluster record when compared with other
major urban dioceses of the East and Midwest. One was economic. In 1859 Bishop John Fitzpatrick (1846–1866) noted in
his diary that despite discrimination against Catholics in
public schools, "It is impossible to open Catholic schools. To
buy lots and erect buildings for this purpose would cost at least
half a million dollars, and then the annual expense for the
support of such schools would be, at the lowest estimate thirty
or forty thousand dollars. Already we find it almost impossible
to provide churches for the hundreds of thousands of poor
people whom the last ten years have sent to our shores. The

50 provision of schools is then plainly impossible."[5]

Bishop Fitzpatrick's reasoning, however, only partially stands up to scrutiny. To be valid it would have to meet two tests: one, that Boston Catholics were poorer than Catholics in dioceses that built schools on a large scale; two, that, even if poorer, their poverty was so extreme that they could not afford schools. The facts seem to indicate that, though actually poorer as a group than their coreligionists elsewhere, they probably could have afforded schools had they really wanted them.

The Irish, who made up the overwhelming bulk of Catholic immigration to Boston until very late in the nineteenth century, came for one reason: the ships they could most easily reach and afford were bound there. But, unfortunately for the Irish, by the time their immigration reached floodtide in the 1840s, Boston had ceased to be a prime employer, at least compared with other American cities. It was never known for labor-intensive industry and had already lost out to New York in the competition for commercial monopolies. The great Boston shipping fortunes amassed in earlier days were now invested elsewhere.

Because of the dearth of opportunities, the immigrants who stayed in Boston tended to be either the relative few who through unusual talent or good luck did well or the many too poor or despondent to move on. What jobs did exist often resulted from an overabundance of labor and the consequent possibility of low wages. Thus the city created public works like the landfill projects on which most of modern Boston stands, and middle-class householders saw the possibility of domestic servants come within reach. By 1850, in a city that boasted 992 distinct occupations, 64 percent of the Irish who were employed worked either as day laborers or as domestic servants. The Irish made up 82 percent of all day laborers and 72 percent of all servants. As one famous Yankee confided, "They keep the price of labor within bounds. . . . If our Southern people could make up their minds to send their slaves back to Africa, this overwhelming immigration . . .

---

5) Memorandum, March 19, 1859, Boston Archdiocesan Archives.

would afford the ready means of filling the vacuum."[6] The Irish were to Boston what the slaves were to the South.

Catholic leaders clearly recognized Boston's disadvantageous position and urged Irish immigrants to move on, founding the Irish Immigrant Society for that purpose in 1847. The *Pilot* complained of the thousands of immigrants "struggling against each other for precarious employment" in the "already crowded streets" of Boston. Going west, said the editor, "should be their thought by day and their dream by night. . . . The East has neither room nor resources for them. . . . Here they are eating the bread out of each others' mouths."[7] Many heeded the advice, hence helping to produce an incredibly high out-migration rate throughout the century, but also leaving those with the fewest resources behind. One might safely conclude that, though poor everywhere, the Catholic urban immigrants of the nineteenth century were probably poorest in Boston.

Although they were poor, the evidence suggests that they were not too poor to build and support parochial schools.

For example, the money spent on the Ursuline convent school in the 1820s and 1830s, which educated primarily the daughters of prominent Protestants, and the building of Holy Cross College in the 1840s, which from its country setting in Worcester appealed to Catholic boys throughout the United States, could have supported eleven primary school teachers at the Boston public school salary rate for twenty years, the length of Bishop Fenwick's tenure. Thus the same money could have provided an elementary school education for ten times the number of students educated at the Ursuline convent and Holy Cross College combined.

But Bishop Fenwick, a southern aristocrat descended from an old Maryland Catholic family and trained in the elitist Jesuit tradition, never seemed to comprehend the educational revolution that had begun to emanate from Massachusetts. Although he professed himself, and genuinely so,

---

6) Edward Everett to N. W. Senior, April 29, 1851, Everett Papers, Massachusetts Historical Society.

7) *Pilot,* March 6, April 15, 1850.

52 dedicated to separate Catholic education and complained of the public schools "under Protestant teachers" using books "teeming with the abuse of Catholics, and with slanders against their religion," and though he even included classrooms for a school in the basement of every Boston church he built, he never quite carried the plan to completion as he did the building of the more select Holy Cross College and the Charlestown convent. Though schools taught by lay teachers opened for brief periods in each of these basement classrooms, none endured. In the press of allocating limited resources, Fenwick chose to educate the elite and settled for an elaborate system of Sunday schools to reach the masses.

Nothing better reveals the curious inability of this otherwise shrewd and capable man to grasp the nature of Boston's common schools than a letter he wrote to the Congregation for the Propagation of the Faith in Paris in 1845: "What we desire most now, and what will ultimately be of the greatest benefit to the Catholic cause, is to provide means for the education of the thousands of Catholic children who are now running wild in the streets of Boston, and who have no other schools to resort to than the Protestant schools already established, and for the support of which our Catholic parents are equally taxed with others." He went on to insist that "of all the evils we have to contend with, this I deem the greatest. . . . Unless some remedy be applied to this evil and applied soon, it will be needless to erect any more churches."[8] One would assume the proposed remedy to be parochial schools. Instead Fenwick outlined his plan for what was to become Boston College. Thus a Jesuit college, albeit this time in the heart of the city, was Fenwick's answer to the Boston public school. One would have to conclude that not poverty alone but priorities that dictated allocation of resources to higher instead of elementary education helped prevent development of a parochial school system during Fenwick's time.

No doubt Boston Catholicism's financial status hit its nadir during the Fitzpatrick administration because of the potato famine immigration. Yet between February and June

---

8) Fenwick to Congregation for the Propagation of the Faith, February 26, 1845, University of Notre Dame Archives.

in Ireland. In the mid-1850s he rebuilt Holy Cross College, which had been destroyed by fire and lacked insurance, and then he completed Fenwick's plan by building Boston College. Both were accomplished largely through collections in the parishes. In 1858 he raised $120,000 for a new orphanage, primarily through donations from the faithful. Yet in 1859 Fitzpatrick contended that to build a parochial school system would be impossible. With a Catholic population in the city of over 80,000, using his own cost estimates, the annual operating expenses would have come to less than $.50 per capita and the schools could have been built at a cost of $6.25 per capita—a heavy but not impossible burden, given the obvious generosity of Boston's impoverished Catholics for other causes. Had the priority been there, the capital costs for buildings could have been kept to a minimum. But the priority seemed to be elsewhere.

Catholic Bostonians had early displayed a penchant for grandiose churches. Through the Fenwick and Fitzpatrick eras (1825–1866), generally modest structures were built, and frequently former Protestant churches in areas where Catholics had displaced Protestants were purchased. Yet the seeds of monumentalism were planted. The first instance was in South Boston at Saints Peter and Paul, built in 1845 "on a scale of magnificence hitherto unparalleled in this region. Crowned by a tower eighty-six feet high," it cost $64,000 at a time when most of its parishioners made a dollar a day if they could find work. The church burned in 1848, and, though underinsured by $25,000, rose from the ashes on an even more impressive scale, "by far the best church in the Diocese at the time, and one of the finest ecclesiastical edifices in the country."[9] This parish had no school until 1860, fifteen years after its founding. Priorities dictated an elegant church before a school.

In Charlestown, long the scene of anti-Catholicism from the destruction of the Ursuline convent in 1834 to the nativist demonstrations of 1847 to the Hannah Corcoran riots of 1853, Catholics took their revenge in 1859 by building a

---

9) Robert H. Lord et al., *History of the Archdiocese of Boston* (Boston: Pilot Publishing Company, 1945), 2:26, 491.

54　church on historic Bunker Hill. So auspicious was the occasion that Archbishop John Purcell came from Cincinnati to lay the cornerstone for "a most beautiful Catholic church, stately raising its spire on a par with Bunker Hill Monument."[10] As beautiful—and defiant—as this Catholic monument on Bunker Hill may have been, it had no school until thirty years after the parish's founding. Parochial schooling once again had been sacrificed to the competition for ever loftier spires.

　　　The mystique of monumentalism did not gain full headway until the postbellum period under the permissive leadership of Archbishop John Williams (1866–1907). Writing in the 1940s, the official archdiocesan historian exulted that "of Catholic churches that existed in Boston in 1866, hardly half a dozen could be regarded as large and impressive. But from the age of Archbishop Williams there have come down to us in this city at least a score of great temples that remain splendid monuments of the zeal of their builders for the glory of the house of God and of the boundless generosity of the faithful."[11] Of these, the one that best symbolized both the glory and folly of Boston Catholicism's reach for architectural grandeur was the new cathedral. Agitation to replace the beautiful but outgrown Bulfinch structure that stood on Franklin Street since 1803 began when Gaetano Bedini visited Boston, as the first apostolic nuncio to the United States, in 1853. Bedini found Boston's Catholic cathedral "a sorrowful contrast to the rest of the splended city."[12] Overwhelmed by the value Americans seemed to place on display of wealth, Bedini concluded that "the huge development of the cities does not allow the Catholics to have modest churches. The majesty, the convenience of external worship, is now a dire necessity lest the Catholics suffer in comparison with the Protestants, who have many beautiful churches. Furthermore, these Cathedrals may stop the preconceived ideas

10) *Pilot,* June 28, 1862.

11) Lord et al., *History,* 3:267.

12) Bedini to Congregation for the Propagation of the Faith, October 8, 1853, in James F. Connelly, *The Visit of Archbishop Gaetano Bedini to the United States of America* (Rome: Gregorian University, 1960), p. 44.

of the rich and influential, who think that poverty is the
exclusive prerogative of Catholics. It is very interesting to
note that Americans usually associate poverty with disgrace."[13]

The bishop did not agree with Bedini's reasoning, but
the latter's appeal to "the vivid desire" of Boston Catholics for
a new cathedral, and his strong recommendation to Rome,
eventually induced Fitzpatrick to sell the old cathedral in
1859, buy property in the newly developing South End, and
hire an architect to plan an edifice suited to Bedini's desires.
But the Civil War and then Fitzpatrick's death intervened.
Completion of the task fell to the new bishop, John
Williams.

Williams devoted himself to this mission, which was to
become his "greatest single achievement."[14] Begun in 1866
and completed in 1875 at a cost of $1.5 million, with a debt
not paid off until 1895, Bedini's dream castle proved a white
elephant even before dedication. The South End site had
been selected in the 1850s, when that section, newly
reclaimed from the sea and replete with broad avenues,
squares, and parks, promised to develop into a prestigious resi-
dential area. But before the cathedral's completion, the
adjoining Back Bay section, where landfill had begun in 1857,
became the showplace of Boston; and the South End swiftly
fell into decline, leaving "one of the noblest religious edifices
in America" stranded. A lack of funds also left the cathedral
truncated—minus the two spires that were to rise two hundred and three hundred feet, respectively, above the posh
South End. The final insult came in the early twentieth century when the Boston elevated ran a line past the cathedral's
front door. The great monument proved less than monumental, despite the effort and expenditure. This church, in the
bishop's own parish, went without a school until 1911, thirty-
six years after its dedication.

The cathedral merely preceded a whole phalanx of
grand churches through the later nineteenth century. Some
of these also had schools nearby. But by 1900, of the twenty-

---

13) Ibid., June 12, 1854, in Connelly, *Visit of Bedini*, p. 213.

14) Lord et al., *History*, 3:54.

56 five Boston parishes without schools, at least 40 percent had built churches on a scale exceeding the parishioners' means. These parishes waited an average of twenty-eight years before building schools. Thus the liberal expenditures on church buildings in Boston tend to belie the contention that Catholics could not afford schools.

The very pattern of building underscores a difference in priority between Boston and other urban dioceses. In Boston, Bishop Fenwick's original policy of building a church with school rooms in the basement gradually evolved into one of first designing a monumental church, then building the basement with available funds and roofing it for church services, and then building the upper church as money came in, a process that took ten to twenty years. One such basement church still raises its stunted head barely above ground level.

By contrast, in some other dioceses, when a new parish was formed and funds were scarce, the school was built first, with an auditorium to be used on Sunday for religious services. The congregation used this over a period of years while raising funds for a permanent church. Nineteenth-century Boston offered only three instances of such church schools, and for the rest completely disregarded the practice. The contrasting architectural practices suggest a drastic difference not in wealth but in priorities.

One is tempted to speculate about what lay behind this difference in economic priorities. Boston Catholics probably leaned toward monumental churches because they offered the only means of impressing their presence on the city. Magnificent churches could be seen for miles around. It mattered that Saint Francis de Sales Church in Charlestown raised its spire "on a par with the Bunker Hill Monument" and that the dome and twin spires of the Mission Church could "dominate the skyline of Roxbury." The fact that Saint Peter's in Dorchester occupied "a commanding eminence" with a 150-foot tower "visible far out to sea" announced to the Yankees that the Irish were in Boston to stay.[15] For a people crushed economically and despised for both their religion and ethnic origins, such visibility became a psychological necessity. The grandiose

---

15) *Pilot,* June 28, 1862; Lord et al., *History,* 3:249–250, 257.

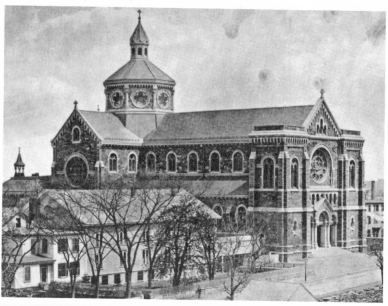

The Mission Church in Roxbury and St. Peter's Church in Dorchester, were among several built in the nineteenth century to let the Yankees know that the Catholics were in Boston to stay.

58   church also established a certain economic respectability. Bedini had understood correctly, after all, that Americans associated poverty with disgrace. Yet in Boston the Irish had remained economically depressed. The financial respectability they could not achieve as individuals could be simulated collectively through their churches. Even the Catholic critics of monumentalism recognized the powerful compulsion to appear affluent. In 1883 *Donahoes' Magazine* advised against too many expensive churches yet recommended "a few great churches to show what we *can* do."[16] In a Yankee society that associated wealth with virtue, a few opulent churches seemed necessary. The squat school churches, utilitarian but ugly, would never do in Boston.

This peculiar yet understandable psychology, which helps explain the Boston Catholic allocation of financial resources, also underscores the extreme degree to which the dominant Yankee traditions generally determined the Catholic course of action. This appears to be the key to understanding Boston Catholic history, at least through the nineteenth century. So strong was the social and moral value system expressed through the flinty New England character and imbedded in its institutions that fundamental developments in Boston Catholicism can only be understood as reactions to that tradition. This was especially true of the Catholic stance toward Boston's public schools, the tradition's cherished guardian.

Boston had a long history of publicly supported education, going back two hundred years before Catholics arrived in any significant numbers. Though suffering periods of neglect in the eighteenth century, it had survived intact, and the Boston Latin School, at least, enjoyed national acclaim. In 1789 a new school law had rejuvenated the Boston schools, and a revision in 1819 led to further development. After 1800 Boston spent almost one-fifth of its tax revenues on public education, and by mid-century its per-pupil expenditures more than doubled those of other American cities. When Horace Mann became the first secretary of the Massachusetts Board of Education, he found the Boston schools already fully

---

16) *Donahoes Magazine* (May 1883): 467.

developed, in contrast to the rest of Massachusetts. Though often criticized by idealistic reformers, throughout the nineteenth century they maintained a reputation as pacemakers nationally. Well before the progressive movement of the early twentieth century, the Boston schools had instituted or experimented with just about every educational reform: kindergarten, manual training, child study, trade and industrial schools, vocational guidance, supervised play and playgrounds, innovation in school design, and the like. Their reputed quality alone made the Boston schools attractive to Catholics.

Nor were Catholic school spokesmen in Boston unaware of this. Indeed they seldom made attempts to promote parochial schools without reference to the public ones. The Catholic press frequently stressed that, except for religion, the Catholic schools taught the same subjects as the public ones, in the same way, and sometimes even with the same textbooks. Rarely were the public schools criticized except for their anti-Catholicism or lack of religious training. The preoccupation with convincing their readers that Catholic schools came up to the public ones was explicit and revealed a clear awareness that public schools stood out as models to emulate. Their quality clearly beckoned to aspiring Catholics, probably to a degree greater than in any other American city at the time.

The schools beckoned for another reason as well. The high quality of Boston's public schools was no accident. It reflected and resulted from the native Bostonian's intense awareness of the venerable Yankee tradition and his concern to conserve and pass it on through the schools. Possibly more than any other city in America Boston had, before the Irish arrived, a homogeneous tradition—Protestant, Anglo-Saxon, New England—in which it took profound, if narrow and even bigoted, pride. "The town had what the French call a solidarity, an almost personal consciousness, rare anywhere, rare especially in America," said poet James Russell Lowell.[17] In the face of alien immigration, the city fathers sought all the

17) James Russell Lowell, *My Study Windows* (Boston: Houghton Mifflin, 1885), p. 95.

60 more to preserve that tradition. They could not, certainly, do it through the aliens' equally alien church. They could not do it through the alien family, uninitiated into even the rudiments of urban living. The public school stood out as the best hope, thus explaining the emphasis on expansion and improvement of public education in nineteenth-century Boston, including the nation's first compulsory school attendance laws.

Despite their obvious distaste for Yankees, the Irish felt a certain need, even without compulsory legislation, to enter through the public school door in hope of initiation into the great tradition and ultimate acceptance. The weight of Boston's history, "these great names, and these awesome institutions was oppressive to the Boston Irish. It could not help but produce in them a massive inferiority complex."[18] But perhaps they could nullify that complex by participation in one of the Yankee's awesome institutions—the public school.

Probably no other Irishman illustrates this strange love-hate relationship with the dominant social system, as well as its perilous consequences, better than the pivotal bishop of the nineteenth century, John Fitzpatrick. A second-generation Irish lad from riot-prone Broad Street, Fitzpatrick's great natural ability won him admission to the Boston Latin school in 1826, where he excelled and met the sons of Boston's best families: the Cabots, Appletons, Lincolns, and the like. Despite his choice of an ecclesiastical career, the friendships he made at Latin, which he cultivated always, gained him access to a world far removed from Broad Street. As a charter member of the Thursday Evening Club, he associated with Boston's foremost intellectuals: Richard Henry Dana, Louis Agassiz, Oliver Wendell Holmes, Abbot Lawrence, Edward Everett, and Francis Parkman, to mention only some of the better known. In 1861 he achieved the ultimate in Yankee acceptance, an honorary degree from Harvard. Years later Henry Cabot Lodge reminisced about his boyhood memories of Bishop Fitzpatrick who had gone to school with his uncle, George Cabot, and "kept up his friendship with our family."

18) William V. Shannon, *The American Irish* (New York: Macmillan, 1963), p. 183.

"He was a most excellent man, very popular and greatly
beloved. He came a great deal to our house in the summer" at
Nahant. He was "genial, affectionate, and sympathetic" and
"very kind to me."[19]

No doubt the natives considered him a prime example
of what they hoped to accomplish through the public
schools—a Yankeefied Irishman. Indeed upon his appointment as bishop, the Boston press paid him the highest possible
tribute: "born in Boston, and in part educated in our public
schools."[20] To all appearances, Fitzpatrick had been completely assimilated.

Yet the private man revealed a different image from that
projected to the Cabot Lodges. After one particularly strong
anti-Irish incident in Boston, he wrote to his sister: "It is
another example of the base spirit of New Englanders. Vile
narrow minded scoundrels . . . They'll drawl long speeches
about liberality and toleration and about the freedom of their
institutions but it would be hard to find a people more void of
honest principles and of every sentiment becoming an honorable man and yet they have the unsupportable vanity to look
upon themselves as the first nation on earth. Spiteful
wretches, I'll not stir up my bile thinking of them any
longer."[21]

Probably no Yankee ever heard this fiery, Irish side of
Fitzpatrick's personality. He had learned to play the game too
well—in public school. But the game required immense control, not only over himself but his entire Catholic following.
Unlike his predecessor, Fitzpatrick was convinced that Catholics could succeed in Boston not by separation but by passive
acquiescence, patiently awaiting a better day. In the Know-
Nothing elections he cautioned Catholics not to object if
their votes were voided on technicalities at the polls. Rather
than risk a confrontation with Hannah Corcoran demonstra-
tors, he called off church services. When riot threatened, he

19) Henry Cabot Lodge, *Early Memories* (New York: Charles Scribner's Sons, 1913), p. 56.

20) *Boston Advertiser*, August 14, 1846.

21) Fitzpatrick to Eleanor Fitzpatrick, January 12, 1838, quoted in Richard J. Gro-
zier, "The Life and Times of John Bernard Fitzpatrick, Third Roman Catholic
Bishop of Boston" (Ph.D. diss.)

sent priests through the streets exhorting Catholics to stay indoors. He advised Archbishop Purcell before the latter's Boston visit to use a little "soft soap" on the Yankees, since "nothing works upon them so effectively as a shew of confidence in their sense of justice."[22] When religious principle forced him to protest blatant discrimination, as in the refusal to allow priests access to Catholic inmates of public institutions or the Protestant bias in public schools, he did so in meek, deferential terms.

The pursuit of peace at almost any price necessarily obviated any strong advocacy of parochial schools, despite indications that he favored them. Instead his policy of appeasement and hopes for a better day swung the balance in favor of public schools. Perhaps through the schools his Catholics could gain acceptance as he had done.

John Williams (1866–1907), Fitzpatrick's successor, though very different in temperament and training, appears to have thought similarly. Like Fitzpatrick, Williams was born of immigrant parents in the Irish North End. But unlike Fitzpatrick, he attended public school for just one year. In 1827, at the age of five, he entered a school for boys recently opened by Bishop Fenwick in the Cathedral basement. Taught exclusively by seminarians and young priests, he came under constant clerical influence. Love for the clerical state determined the rest of Williams's life. As seminarian, priest, and then archbishop, he shunned society. "Reserved, silent, gravely and distantly polite, austere in his life and bearing, retiring, averse to all publicity," he tempted one "to conclude that the chill of New England had frozen his Irish blood."[23]

His impenetrable silence disturbed some contemporaries, and perplexes historians. "One who knew him well and who saw him often was sometimes asked, 'What did he say?' and the answer invariably was, 'What he always says, nothing.'"[24] His letters, all written in his own hand, seldom

---

22) Fitzpatrick to Archbishop John Purcell, August 20, 1859, University of Notre Dame Archives.

23) Lord et al., *History*, 3:427.

24) Reverend Mother Augustine, "Life of Archbishop Williams," manuscript, n.d., Boston Archdiocesan Archives. Mother Augustine was the daughter of Samuel Tuckerman, a prominent Bostonian who converted to Catholicism. She had known Williams from her childhood.

The Most Reverend John J. Williams, Archbishop of Boston from 1866–1907, displayed much of the same ambivalence towards parochial schools as his predecessors.

went more than four lines and often consisted simply of a "yes" or "no." Further, "It was not his custom to give reasons for his actions."[25] Thus this sphinxlike figure casts a mysterious pall over his forty-year tenure of the Boston diocese. He was considered the "nestor" of the American hierarchy, yet he seldom spoke out on anything.

25) *Boston Herald,* quoted in *Guidon* (September 1907).

64   Nevertheless certain conclusions can be drawn from Williams's actions and the few words he left behind. One is that he lacked enthusiasm for parochial schools. During his first ten years, he did nothing about them. Early reports to Rome state simply that most Catholic children attended public school. But in the late 1870s he came under fire in his own diocese from a group of clergymen called "the schoolmen." When one of them excommunicated parents for not supporting the parish school, and the matter reached the public press, Williams was compelled to speak. At a clergy conference, he advocated the building of parochial schools but in general enough terms that no clergyman felt compelled to begin immediately. He also denied the right of individual pastors to excommunicate parishioners who sent their children to public school. When Rome learned of the issue and asked why Boston had no parochial school system, he replied that it was being built. But the statistics indicated no substantial change. Records show his active involvement in recruiting sisters and brothers for charitable works, but the quest for religious teachers was left to others. Though Protestant Boston took alarm at the Third Council of Baltimore's mandate to build a school in every parish, Williams implemented the council's decree "somewhat tardily and incompletely."[26] Though appointing a school board in 1889 and a superintendent in 1897, he still left schools to originate solely from initiative at the parish level. He thought well of Archbishop Ireland's plan for accommodation with public education in Minnesota and refused to sign a letter proposed by Archbishop Corrigan condemning it, though characteristically staying out of the fracas that erupted among the American hierarchy in 1892 over the issue. Cardinal Gibbons reported that Williams's "wish would be to submit the schools of his diocese to a similar arrangement." But no record exists that he tried.[27]

26) Lord et al., *History*, 3:336.

27) Cardinal Simeoni to Williams, November 21, 1891, with Williams's notation in margin, "think well of them," Boston Archdiocesan Archives; Williams to Corrigan, April 11, 1892, Boston Archdiocesan Archives; Cardinal Gibbons to Pope Leo XIII, March 1, 1892, Baltimore Diocesan Archives, in Robert Emett Curran, "Michael Augustine Corrigan and the Shaping of Conservative Catholicism in America, 1878–1895" (Ph.D. diss., Yale University, 1974).

Williams seldom approached the Yankee world. He preferred a low profile for himself and for other Catholics in Boston as well. Though his flock had achieved a numerical majority in Boston by century's end and was poised to take it over politically, Williams seemed still cowed by the Yankee ideology and institutions. Psychologically he still lived in the Boston of his youth when, as he put it nostalgically at the golden jubilee of his priesthood, "I knew all the Catholics of the City—they all went to one church."[28] His critics complained that "Archbishop Williams was too self-effaced, too passive, too silent, too timid, and that the Church was quite too long and too unnecessarily hiding in the catacombs."[29] But life in the catacombs seemed to be the price Williams was willing to pay if he could avoid the combat he shunned. To have launched a strong parochial school effort, for instance, would certainly have provoked battle.

The Yankees also had to pay a price to maintain their schools triumphant. On the one hand, to safeguard the future of their society, they wanted Catholic children in public schools. Thus speaking of Irish immigrants and their proclivity to liquor, one prominent Bostonian in 1852 took comfort in the fact that "the children are sent to our free public schools, and the second generation comes out much improved."[30] With a population almost half-Catholic already, attracting these children to public school seemed all the more imperative. On the other hand, it appeared that in order to keep the public schools acceptable to Catholics, certain concessions would have to be made. Here was the dilemma facing the guardians of Yankee tradition: to keep the schools as conveyors of the full Puritan tradition would make them unacceptable to Catholics, but to change them, in particular to abandon their Protestant flavor as a means of attracting Catholics, would dilute, and perhaps destroy, the very essence of that tradition. The city fathers, and especially those who sat on the school committee, grappled with that dilemma

---

28) Bernard Corr, ed., *Souvenir of the Sacerdotal Golden Jubilee of the Most Reverend Ino J. Williams, D.D., Archbishop of Boston* (Boston, 1895).

29) Lord et al., *History*, 3:428.

30) Edward Everett to the Duchess of Argyle, February 3, 1852, Everett Papers.

through the nineteenth century in a kind of constant battle both to maintain the cultural purity of the schools and to keep them acceptable to Catholics. The struggle crystalized in several specific incidents, and each time the resolution involved sufficient concession to keep the schools at least minimally acceptable. Grudging as their compromises may have been, the Yankees refused to slam the public school door on Catholics. This fact no doubt also helps explain the Catholics' ambivalence toward the necessity of parochial schooling.

Bishop Fenwick precipitated the first such incident in 1843 when he wrote a letter to Mayor Martin Brimmer, an ex officio member of the Boston School Committee, complaining about an anti-Catholic bias in public school textbooks. He singled out Worcester's *Elements of History—Ancient and Modern* for particular comment, claiming that "after having attentively perused its pages I unhesitatingly say that it is not such a Book as should be put into the hands of children of any Denomination of Christians who are desirous of being correctly instructed in history and much less into the hands of the Catholic youth of this city, whose religious tenets it unsparingly assails, whose morality, as taught by their church, it takes every opportunity to impugn, and whose best men it everywhere holds up as superstitious and ignorant." Fenwick also charged that "several other schoolbooks . . . are liable to the same objections," and he concluded with a polite, but thinly veiled threat: "We have at this present moment many thousands of children frequenting the public schools who will have, much to our regret, to be withdrawn from them in the event of the evil here complained of not being immediately remedied."

Fenwick sent a much lengthier letter directly to the school committee, outlining in detail his objections to both Worcester's history and other books used in the schools. The matter was referred to the committee on books, which reported two months later: "Your committee have a high opinion of Worcester's *Elements of History*. If there were none but the children of Protestants in our schools, we should never had been called upon to inquire into its fitness as a textbook." After several other clearly hostile statements that "we should reject with indignation the idea of presenting garbled statements of facts, or of suppressing truths which ought to be told in an historical work," the committee did grudgingly admit that "the allegations against it amount to little more than this, that it treats the points at issue between Catholics and Protestants in a Protestant spirit. To this charge your committee think that it is justly liable." In fact, the committee admitted that the book probably violated the law, and recommended that one chapter and several passages be dropped from the text. The school committee adopted the recommendation but ignored Fenwick's complaints about the other books.[31] Thus it resolved this issue by grudging tokenism. Though the solution did not satisfy Fenwick, he made no attempt to remove Catholic children from the schools.

The second incident, more dramatic, occurred in 1859, and came to be known as the Eliot school case. An Irish Catholic boy, Thomas Wall, had been suspended from school for refusing to recite the Protestant version of the Ten Commandments, claiming his father had forbidden it. The issue escalated when the local priest told all the Catholic boys to follow Wall's example. They complied, and the school was in turmoil for days. In the meantime, after his father's conference with the school's principal, Wall had been reinstated. He was again told to recite the commandments, and again refused. As the presumed instigator, he was then beaten by his teacher on the palms of his hands until they bled; and, after somewhere between twenty and thirty minutes of this treatment, he gave in and recited the Ten Commandments. The incident created great excitement, and Wall's parents sued the alleged child beater, who was acquitted after a much publicized trial on grounds that he had merely enforced the law.

The issue also prompted much debate on the Boston School Committee. Significantly a solid majority agreed that the boy should not have been forced to recite the objectionable commandments. But a majority also maintained that the issue should have been resolved by bringing it to the school committee, not by public demonstration and open defiance of

---

31) Fenwick to Brimmer, January 28, February 23, 1843; Brimmer to Fenwick, April 5, 1845, Boston Archdiocesan Archives; Boston School Committee, minutes, February 7, March 7, April 4, 1843, Boston Public Library.

68   the law. It was therefore agreed that the committee would stand by the school and the offending teacher, and then, once emotions had quieted, change the law. Within the year they did exactly that, making it illegal to force any child to recite anything contrary to his religious principles.

The new regulation, however, did not ban either the reading of the Protestant Bible or the recitation of the Protestant version of the Lord's prayer and Ten Commandments. It merely made it possible for Catholic children and other dissenters to refrain from participation. The guardians of tradition had made just enough compromise to keep the public schools tolerable for Catholics without sacrificing their essential Yankee flavor.

The third incident, in 1888, began in a manner similar to those in 1843 and 1859, but, due to social and political changes over the intervening years, it ended somewhat differently. A teacher at the Boston English High School, Charles B. Travis, had defined an indulgence as "a permission to commit sin" that was "sometimes bought with money." He persisted in this teaching even after objections from a Catholic student. A Catholic pastor protested to the school committee. At a hearing, Travis argued that he had merely taught what the approved text said. But the school committee dropped the textbook, censured Travis publicly, and assigned him to teach ancient history instead. The harsh, swift treatment differed markedly from the school committee's reluctant, carefully measured concession to Catholics in 1843 and 1859. The difference stemmed in part from the fact that the 1888 committee was half-Catholic; those of 1843 and 1859 had been entirely Protestant.

The school committee's action triggered a public response that reflected anxieties building up for forty years. Previously Catholics had meekly sought redress for perceived wrongs in the public schools. Now they seemed to some to be dictating public school policy according to their own religious tenets. Many Bostonians saw in the committee's decision the first clear sign that "in the future the Pope, and not the American people, must select the textbooks for the schools."[32]

---

32) *British American Citizen*, quoted in *Pilot*, June 23, 1888.

The fears of Yankee Bostonians focused not merely on domination of the school committee. Since the early 1850s, the naturalization of Irish Catholic immigrants had posed an increasing threat to Protestant hegemony. In 1857 the first Irish Catholic was elected to the city council, in 1859 the first school committee member, and in 1870 the first alderman. During the 1870s Irish Catholics moved in large numbers onto the police force, fire department, city council, and school committee. Finally, in 1884, Bostonians elected Hugh O'Brien their first Irish mayor. Although not the machine politician of later times, he closed the public library on St. Patrick's day, symbolizing a sharp break from Puritan tradition. When Travis was censured in 1888, O'Brien sat in the mayor's office and Catholics served as chairman of the board of aldermen, as president of the common council, and as chairman of the school committee.

Until 1888 the progressive Irish takeover had been staunchly opposed yet accepted with stoic resignation. But the Travis affair triggered a severe backlash that produced a last-ditch, temporarily successful stand to retrieve Boston from the Irish. The united efforts of numerous anti-Catholic organizations, spearheaded by the British Americans and several evangelical Protestant ministers, focusing on the forthcoming elections, drove O'Brien from office and swept city hall almost clean of Irishmen. Because only one-third of the school committee's members were chosen each year, it took three years to reclaim the Boston School Committee fully. By 1890, with Catholic representation reduced to a nominal two out of twenty-four, the committee, now dominated by militant anti-Catholics, adopted two history texts said to be even more prejudiced than the one dropped in 1888.

The fury of the effort and the fact that it took a Travis incident to trigger it underscored the immense weight that many Protestant Bostonians placed on the public schools as the guardian of their future. The Catholics might take over police and fire departments and even city hall without violent reaction, but never the public schools. Yet the backlash and its vengeful, repressive triumph also produced a reaction that alarmed more moderate Bostonians. So complete and final did the defeat seem to the Catholics that its organ, the *Pilot*, for the first time launched a crusade for parochial schools. "Common self respect," argued the editor, compelled "the withdrawal of Catholic children from schools in which it has been officially decreed that they have no rights which Protestants are bound to respect. . . . Multiply the Catholic schools!"[33]

This stance is not what the guardians of tradition wanted. Concerned as their forebears had been that the schools remain open to all, and especially to those most in need of assimilation, they rallied to the cause of justice for Catholics in the city's public schools. Largely through the Citizens Public School Union, they successfully initiated a compromise on the textbook issue; every history classroom was supplied with supplementary texts presenting modern history from both the Protestant and Catholic points of view. Students were allowed and even encouraged to read both sides. Thus, ironically, religious strife in the schools ushered in a liberal curricular reform far ahead of its time. The Public School Union also helped establish a better religious and ethnic balance on the school committee during the 1890s, leading the way in support of moderates from both sides.

Although the Travis incident and its aftermath resulted in a spate of new parochial schools and though some Catholic spokesmen remained suspicious of the new history program as long as most high school teachers were Protestant, still, as in 1843 and 1859, the schools remained basically acceptable to most Catholics.

On balance, the failure to develop a full-scale parochial school system in Boston probably resulted from an intricate combination of factors. The greater poverty among Catholics in Boston relative to those elsewhere may have played a part. More likely, the failure could be related to the choice of economic priorities, such as a preference for educating the elite that was especially noticeable in the antebellum period and a predilection for grandiose churches in vogue after the Civil War. The results were also heavily influenced by Boston's ecclesiastical leadership. Although devoted to Catholic education and fiercely opposed to "Hereticks," Benedict Fen-

---

wick's southern aristocratic background and experience as a 71
Jesuit influenced his favoring higher education at the expense
of parochial schools. John Fitzpatrick apparently preferred
parochial schools to public, but his timidity in the face of
financial difficulty within and opposition without led him to
think them impossible. The enigmatic John Williams clearly
lacked enthusiasm for parochial schools, neither promoting
them very strongly nor opposing their development.

Initiative at the parish level did lead to the building of many parochial schools such as in St. Thomas Aquinas parish in Jamaica Plain
which opened this building in 1890.

This noncommittal stance during both the Fitzpatrick and Williams administrations threw the responsibility to others. All parochial educational growth after 1846 came from initiative at the parish level, mostly from the clergy. The Jesuits ran both parishes that had schools in 1846. They recruited the Sisters of Notre Dame, who taught every parochial school in Boston until 1873, when a diocesan priest brought in the Sisters of St. Joseph. The bishops sanctioned all this but took no initiative themselves. Certain parish priests emerged as champions of parochial schools. James Fitton developed four parishes in East Boston with schools and no monumental churches. Thomas Scully, spokesman for the schoolmen among the clergy, had a huge school in his Cambridgeport parish complete with marching bands, debating societies, and a gymnasium. Nevertheless many of the other clergy dragged their feet.

Laymen appeared as ambivalent about parochial schools as their clergy did. Although one group complained to Rome about Bishop Fitzpatrick's inaction and the generally lay-controlled *Pilot* routinely endorsed the orthodox parochial school policy, no groundswell ever developed for parochial schools. Only once did the *Pilot* campaign militantly for the building of parochial schools in Boston—after the 1888 controversy seemed to diminish chances of fairness to legitimate Catholic interests in the public schools. But the campaign subsided as moderation took hold again in the Boston School Committee.

The less than enthusiastic devotion to parochial schooling could have been due to the overwhelming Irish predominance in Catholic Boston. By 1907, forty-two of the fifty-three parishes, containing 80 percent of the city's Catholics, were Irish controlled. The Italians had five parishes and 15 percent of the Catholics, while the remaining 5 percent belonged to single parishes run by the Portuguese, French, Poles, Lithuanians, Syrians, and Germans. In earlier decades, the Irish had predominated even more overwhelmingly. Until 1873, they controlled every parish except the single German one founded in 1844. Thus unlike most other northern cities, through the important formative years of the nineteenth century, Boston did not have a truly multiethnic Catholic population.

This fact appears to have militated against the development of a parochial school system in several ways. First, the absence of a large foreign-language Catholic population removed one major impetus for parochial schooling. Elsewhere many foreign language Catholics supported parochial schools as much for preservation of the native language as for their religion, especially since the Church allowed each ethnic group to have its own institutions. But the vast majority of Boston Catholics, being Irish, already spoke English as their mother tongue. Second, the absence of a large German Catholic population removed a more specific impetus from the parochial school movement in Boston. In most other American cities with heavy Catholic concentrations, Germans arrived in large numbers simultaneously with the Irish. The Germans had an intense desire to preserve the native language and, reinforced by a tradition brought from Europe, immediately built schools. Their devotion to parochial schooling in turn evoked a spirit of emulation in the Catholic community. In other cities Irish parishes strove to keep up with German in the competition for institutional excellence, which Germans defined as including a school. But in Boston the single German parish, though boasting a school from its inception, seemed more a novelty than a model to be followed. Third, Boston's largest foreign-language group—the Italian—also lacked interest in parochial schools. Throughout the country, bishops complained that the Italian immigrants did not frequent the Catholic schools. Actually in Boston two of their five parishes did have schools by 1907, but it was hardly a proportion to set the pace for others. Fourth, except for the Italians, and to an extent the Germans, the other foreign-language groups remained so small that maintaining separate institutions, especially schools, proved difficult. Many parishioners did not live near the single church. They may have been able and willing to travel considerable distances to Sunday religious services, but they were reluctant to send their children so far to school every day. By 1907, aside from the one German and two Italian schools, only the Poles

74   provided separate education for their children. In all, only four of the eleven foreign-language parishes in Boston had schools, hardly a model for the Irish to imitate.

Left to their own resources, the Boston Irish never quite made up their minds about parochial schooling. Many seemed more preoccupied with achieving some degree of respectability, and, as one pastor put it in 1895, "Parents think their children will have greater success in life, and obtain positions more easily if they have gone through a public school."[34] One widely read advocate of parochial schools, the *Sacred Heart Review* published in Cambridge, chastised the many Catholics who submitted to "the popular, but very mistaken notion . . . that the public schools are superior to parish schools, and that the education of the former opens up a fairer prospect of worldly advantage than the latter."[35] As yet sketchy evidence does suggest that parochial schools appeared least attractive to those Irish Catholics most aspiring to the middle class in Boston.

The burden of habit also played a part. From the beginning, very few Catholic Bostonians had attended parochial schools. No tradition existed. The parents, if they grew up in Boston, had gone to public school. The same was true of the leaders. Of the 154 prominent Irish men listed in 1893 by James B. Cullen's *The Story of the Irish in Boston* as having gone to school in Boston, only seven had attended a parochial school, and four of these for only part of their elementary schooling. The parochial schools had played an insignificant role in the development of nineteenth-century Boston Irish leadership, though the private Catholic colleges had emerged as increasingly significant. By 1893 almost 14 percent of Boston's prominent Irish males had attended a Catholic college, at least for a time, the great majority of them at Boston College. This no doubt reflected, and perhaps justified, the early hierarchy's emphasis on higher education. But it did not indicate a direct Catholic alternative to the public school.

34) *Annals,* Sisters of Notre Dame, St. Augustine parish, Archives of the Sisters of Notre Dame, Ipswich, Massachusetts.

35) *Pilot,* February 22, 1890, p. 13.

This remained wanting. Its absence can best be understood
against the background of the overwhelming Yankee tradition, stronger probably in Boston than anywhere. For the
Irish, the need to achieve Yankee respectability, and at the
same time express defiance, helped shift precious financial
resources into monumental churches, while the need to move
from the segregated enclaves of Boston into participation in
the dominant culture led many into the public school. For the
Yankees, the need to pass on their treasured way of life intact
led to their intense emphasis on the public schools; and,
above all, the necessity of reducing the threat from these
aliens by absorbing them, dictated keeping the public schools
acceptable to all. Significantly, in Boston large-scale expansion of parochial schools did not take place until after 1907,
when the Irish had already taken control of the city and could
snub the vaunted Yankee heritage.

CHAPTER 5

*Reform and
the Struggle for
Control,
1870–1900*

SAM BARNES

Between 1870 and 1900 Boston's schools would see many Progressive reforms, such as the encouragement of fresh-air activities, often instituted for very conservative reasons.

Boston in the 1870s was a city confronting change. The burgeoning Irish population were no longer newcomers. They had organized their wards into effective political organizations that could often swing an election. In 1879, Irish-born Hugh O'Brien was elected chairman of the board of aldermen, and in 1884 he was the first Irishman to be elected mayor. The unquestioned Yankee rule of the political apparatus had been successfully challenged.

At the same time Boston was confronting the realities of rapid urbanization: crowded tenements, increased crime, widespread disease and poverty, and an ever-growing population. The political, social, and economic institutions of the traditional leadership could not meet the challenges of the new urban America. The Irish political machine was becoming an alternate source of political power. Working men and women were forming unions in an effort to gain economic security. In Boston, there were 550 strikes in the turbulent 1870s.

Against this backdrop, Boston brahmins responded. Many old Boston families tried to isolate themselves by moving out to the suburbs. Others moved into an aristocratic enclave in the new Back Bay and enjoyed an anglophile renaissance. Still others looked to social reform. This reform movement was to have many forms and a duration of close to forty years. A significant part of that movement centered around schools because its leaders viewed education as a means to social improvement and thus social transformation of both the newcomers and the older working-class population.

Several strands of social reform coalesced in the so-called progressive movement in the 1890s. The kindergarten movement and the development of manual training in the schools were two that were important in Boston.

The Kindergarten Movement

The kindergarten movement was the first of the reform movements to surface in Boston and is a good example of the link between social and educational reform. It began in Boston in the 1870s among upper-class women who were concerned about the degradation of city life and its impact on children. Several of the leaders, notably Elizabeth Peabody, had visited the kindergartens in Germany and become acquainted with the educational theory of Friedrich Froebel, the mentor of kindergartens.

Annie Fields, a Boston philanthropist, expresses this view:

> "Let us take the little child in the future from its possible ignorant, filthy, and careless mother as soon as it can walk and give it three hours daily where during that time it will be made clean, will enjoy light, color, order, and music and the sweet influence of a living and self-controled voice."

Kindergartens were seen as a way to remove children from the evil and immoral influences of tenement life and place them in an environment in which their true spirit could surface and be nurtured. The kindergarten crusade received an additional boost from the fledgling child-study movement, which, like Froebel, saw the first seven years as the key to a child's development. In 1880 G. Stanley Hall, a psychologist who later became president of Clark University in Worcester, published a study entitled "Contents of Children's Minds." He had studied children entering the Boston public schools and found that urban children were "more ignorant" than rural children, that immigrant children were "more ignorant" than native children, and that children who attended kindergarten did much better than those who did not. Thus advocates argued that kindergartens seemed important not only in terms of moral development; but they helped to prepare children for further schooling.

The first kindergartens in Boston were privately supported and located in the poorer sections of the city. They followed a social settlement model and saw their purpose as both uplifting the children and using them as a means to regenerate the entire community. The main financial backer and advocate for the kindergarten movement in Boston was Pauline Agassiz Shaw, who between 1882 and 1888 contributed $200,000 to thirty-one kindergartens throughout the city. One of her most famous was in the North End, a crowded immigrant neighborhood. The kindergarten teachers spent a large portion of their time visiting the children in their homes

Pauline Agassiz Shaw, wealthy Yankee benefactor of Boston's kindergarten movement.

and attempting to influence the families to place cleanliness, morality, and temperance as high priorities. Kindergartens were seen as the opening wedge to bring order and Yankee morality to children, who would then bring it into the home and the street.

Responding to the same uncertainties in city life as the later settlement houses, the kindergarten received important support from settlement house advocates. Robert A. Woods, founder of the South End Settlement House in Boston, saw the kindergarten as an important force: "The Kindergarten makes the child a social being. Acts of self-denial, self-control, and courtesy, or regard for the rights of others, and the respect for property teach the child to yield his individual will for the good of the many."[1]

In 1888, Shaw's private kindergartens were taken over by the city. This pattern of private initiation and financing of educational reform has been an important one in Boston. A number of the educational reforms of the late nineteenth and early twentieth centuries followed the pattern. Since it was in the political arena that the traditional power of Yankees was being challenged, reform through the public sector was more difficult. Those with the money, and a belief in their role as educational leaders, initiated many programs on a private basis and later handed them over to the school department to continue and expand.

In 1888 when the kindergartens were taken over, Edwin Seaver was superintendent of schools; he was also a supporter of the broader social reform concept of kindergarten: "The kindergarten offers a much needed protection from the injurious influence of the street. For those unfortunate children—and there are many who suffer from parental carelessness, indifference, ignorance, or poverty, the kindergarten measurably supplies what the home does not—kindly nurture in the virtues and graces of a more refined and elevated democratic life."[2]

The public schools carried on much of the community outreach that had been an integral part of the Shaw kindergartens. Home visits were continued as part of the kindergarten teachers' duties. They would teach in the mornings, visit the homes in the afternoon, and have meetings with mothers on subjects such as health care or sanitation.

Because the number of kindergartens was increasing, the problem arose of training for kindergarten teachers and

1) Robert A. Woods, *The City Wilderness* (Boston: Houghton Mifflin, 1898), p. 236.

2) Quoted in Marvin Lazerson, *Origins of the Urban School: Public Education in Massachusetts, 1870–1915* (Cambridge: Harvard University Press, 1971), p. 58.

the need to establish a kindergarten curriculum. But the kin- dergarten movement had brought together many strains of thought united around the necessity of early childhood education, and it was not easy to reach a unified curriculum. In fact by the 1890s the movement had split over curriculum issues. Some felt that the emancipation of the child should be the central goal, and others felt that it should be uniformity and control. Kindergarten curriculum eventually became quite structured with a methodology for play activity, which served as a model for the larger society. In 1890 the Boston School Committee set up rules for kindergarten, and the teacher-to-pupil ratio was set at one to twenty-five. An instructor was hired at the Boston Normal School to teach early childhood education, and kindergarten was on its way to becoming an accepted part of the American educational experience.

In 1905 Boston had ninety-eight kindergartens with 188 teachers, and over 5,000 pupils. Kindergarten served children from three and a half to five years of age and was attended on a voluntary basis. By 1910 the school department had dropped the social service function of kindergarten, presumably for economic reasons, and teachers were no longer allowed to make home visits or organize mothers' meetings. Thus the notion of early childhood education as a means of reversing the cycles of poverty and ignorance went into partial eclipse for half a century, until it was rediscovered by those who were initiating Head Start programs in the 1960s.

Manual Training

The industrial revolution had begun to make itself felt in New England life before the Civil War, but in the postwar decades the full force of the changes in people's lives became evident. Prewar children were commonly apprenticed to local mechanics to learn both a trade and a fair amount of the community's mores. Postwar children worked in mills employing hundreds and had neither the opportunity to understand how the product was made nor the individual instruction in the ways of society. He or she learned one task and did it. Industrialization thus caused a major dislocation in the integrated educational process of family, church, and work place. The old common school of Horace Mann's day had focused on

82 moral growth and literacy; it did not include mechanical or manual training. The new disharmony of urban, industrial life was a major challenge for the public school system, whose planners used the myth of the recreation of an integrated educational experience to further their mission.

The Philadelphia Exhibition of 1876 provided a model for American educators. The Russian delegation had an exhibit displaying the work of students in their newly organized mechanical arts workshops. Victor Della Vos, who had organized these workshops in St. Petersburg, was present at the exhibition and met several Massachusetts educators visiting the exhibition. They immediately seized the idea of workshops as a model, a way to integrate the mental discipline of manual work with that of academic work.

Manual training, as the movement was called, could instill in children the discipline and respect for work that seemed to have been lost when children moved from being apprentices in the workshop to scholars in the classroom. In Boston, the first major report on manual education appeared in 1883, and the school committee allocated $2,500 in the same year for classes in manual education to be held in the basement of the Latin School. Edwin Seaver, the superintendent of schools, saw it as an important educational strategy: "The city has merely filled with more book learning the gap left by the departed home employments. The traditional balance between learning and labor has been upset, and learning has taken the whole time."[3] Manual training was to fill this gap. Students at all levels of schooling—kindergarten, elementary, and high schools—would spend a few hours a week learning manual skills. These courses were not designed to train them for particular trades or jobs but to develop some skills in the manual and mechanical arts and to experience work as related to learning. The manual training movement had a similar ideology to the kindergarten movement, and many of the backers of the kindergarten were also advocates of manual training. Similarly social reformers such as Robert Woods saw manual training as a way to restore appropriate work values in tenement children. Woods wrote:

3) Ibid., p. 98.

Manual Training for girls in a Boston school.

Manual training is corrective and uplifting. If street and gang life tend to make boys irresponsible and destructive then there is specially needed in the tenement house neighborhoods some interesting work. Children left to their natural impulses, provided they have materials always turn to making things. Manual training is a specific. It stimulates the dormant creative impulses, which in turn supplant the destructive tendencies.[4]

As Woods viewed it, manual training would draw out the best side of the city's poorest children.

Manual training was also a response to deeper problems in public education. The schools had grown considerably during this period. In 1846 there were 17,110 students; in 1880 there were 50,412. Boston had grown not only in terms of population but also in area. By 1890 Charlestown, Dorchester, Roxbury, Brighton, and West Roxbury had been annexed by the city. Compulsory education had been in effect for thirty years. In the early nineteenth century, public education had been an elite institution serving only those whose families

4) Woods, *City Wilderness*, p. 238.

84   could afford to have their children out of work for a number of years. However, by 1880 the schools were becoming an institution that served a large number of working-class children; public education was becoming a mass institution.

But problems with absenteeism and the relevance of curriculum began to emerge. In 1883, the same year that manual training was introduced into the curriculum, the committee on examinations of the Boston School Committee issued a report on the success of the schools:

> Whereas, it is well known fact that the majority of pupils in the grammar schools are withdrawing from them before graduating, and are thereby deprived of sufficient knowledge of the necessary branches of learning which is expected to prepare them for their after life in the world.
>
> Whereas, there is no reason to believe that the graduates of the grammar Schools are not as well grounded in the essential and practical useful studies as were graduates of earlier years. Be it Ordered that: the Committee on Textbooks be instructed when preparing their up coming annual report on the course of studies and the list of textbooks, take serious consideration and report accordingly on the advisability of simplifying the course of study in the Boston Public Schools.[5]

In the annual report of the same year, the school committee addressed the discipline problem: "The unruly element which comes only to find amusement in creating disturbances has been almost excluded entirely by improved management; and much less teacher time is consequently wasted in controlling noisy and troublesome pupils."[6]

The conclusion was that the curriculum of the past was no longer meeting the needs of most of the pupils. The school committee asked that it be revised. Manual training became part of the curriculum in all schools, and educators, politicians, and businessmen began to ponder the question of what sort of schools would be most useful for them.

---

5) Boston School Committee, *Report of Committee on Examinations* (1883).

6) Boston School Committee, *Annual Report* (1883).

Educational reformers considered ways to make the
curriculum more relevant to the new immigrant population.
If the schools were to prepare children to function in American society, then they should be preparing them for the different jobs and tasks that they would confront as adults. But this new task created a multitude of questions and problems. The schools were still functioning on the common school ideology of Horace Mann. The overall curriculum was the same for all schools. Manual education did not mean that only some students received it. In fact the theory was that all students should receive both manual and academic training. In addition, large numbers of students were dropping out of school and therefore missing both the academic and the manual training experience.

In 1904 a study was done following the students who had entered the first grade in 1892. Of the 10,721 entering the first grade, only 6,927 completed primary school (third grade). By the end of elementary school in 1900, only 3,457 remained in the class. By 1904, of the 2,306 who entered high school in 1900, only 559 graduated. The most telling figures are the large dropout rates in primary and elementary school. The small number of students going on to secondary school serves to underline the elite nature of secondary school education. Frequently those who continued secondary school were from the middle- and upper-class families, who sent their children to the Latin School.

Industrial Education

The inclusion of academic courses with the mechanical arts had always been essential to the ideology of the manual training movement. The goal had been to inculcate values and mental disciplines through work as opposed to the techniques of a specific job. But by the 1890s the educational focus of manual training was questioned by people who wanted schools to train students for specific jobs. Much of the support for industrial education, as this new movement came to be called, came from such newly formed organizations as the National Association of Manufacturers and the National Chamber of Commerce. The leaders of business and industry wanted the public education system to be restructured to serve

The North Bennett Street Industrial School, still in operation in the North End.

their needs. In Boston, pressure was put on the North Bennett Street Industrial School to alter its program to emphasize the teaching of trades instead of manual skills. The Mechanical Arts High School, which had been founded in 1893, also came under attack for being too academic. Its original pro-

gram had included not only drawing, carpentry, woodwork-
ing, pattern making, forging, and machine shop practices but
also math, history, science, and a foreign language. The curriculum thus represented the mixture of subjects essential to
the manual training ideology. Before the turn of the century,
however, the demands of industrial education tended to dis-
place the less technical parts of the curriculum.

The move from manual to industrial education was a
major shift in educational priorities and one in which there
was certainly not unanimity. The main questions that arose
were who would decide what the new industrial education
would be, who would be directed toward industrial as opposed
to academic programs, and what would happen to the traditional role of labor unions in the training of their member-
ship. Was educational opportunity being increased or reduced
by creating a school system that offered different programs to
different children?

A major supporter of industrial education in Massachusetts was Frank Leavitt. He had been one of the first
manual education teachers in the Boston schools and had
gone on to become a professor of industrial education at the
University of Chicago. He wrote:

> Industrial education, manual education for industrial
> purposes, recognizes that all cannot have and do not
> need the same education. It means a thorough revision
> of our school system with the purposes of furnishing for
> the working classes an education which bears some-
> what the same relation to their prospective life work as
> does a college education to the future of the profes-
> sional and managerial classes. It means in the final
> analysis the fitting of a particular boy for a particular job
> and it is therefore strongly individualistic. [7]

The debate over industrial education reached the state
level in Massachusetts in 1905 when Governor William L.
Douglas, a shoe manufacturer, appointed the Commission on
Industrial and Technical Education (Douglas Commission).
The commission was to investigate the educational needs of

---

7) Lazerson, *Origins of the Urban School*, p. 134.

88 the various industries in the commonwealth, how well these needs were being met, and what educational programs might meet those needs. The commission was the turning point for vocational education in the commonwealth, and its hearings became a battleground for debate over the merits of industrial education.

The commission members were primarily businessmen and bankers who felt that the public education system should meet the training needs of industry. When they held hearings throughout the state in the fall of 1905, the various sides lined up. The progressive settlement-house movement aligned with the manufacturers and businessmen in favor of teaching the trades within the public school system. On the other side were the numerous labor organizations, which were against the public school system taking over their role as coordinators of apprenticeship training.

Speakers for the industrialists argued that they needed more skilled workers, who could take on the roles of foremen and superintendents. Charles Bosworth, of the Smith and Wesson Company in Springfield, used a nationalist argument to plead for the state funding of industrial training: "We are going to be confronted, as a nation, with the competition of Germany. . . . Then there is Japan. . . . Our hope for the future lies in the superiority of our products and in the training of our workmen."[8] Experts from England familiar with the more advanced English training schools who were brought in to testify portrayed industrial education as the key to the industrial advancement of Europe.

Robert Woods, the social reform advocate and first director of the South End Settlement House, testified in favor of industrial education, linking it to employment needs of manufacturing concerns in the commonwealth. Woods was also concerned with industrial training of a less advanced nature, which could help the poor improve their condition. Other social agencies, including the YMCA, joined Woods in their support of industrial training, pointing out that they had successful extensive evening programs, which offered courses.

8) Massachusetts Commission on Industrial and Technical Education, *Hearings*, November 3, 1905.

The Massachusetts trade unions by and large were against the teaching of trades in the public schools. Frank Foster of the Massachusetts branch of the American Federation of Labor testified against the use of taxpayers' money to break up the apprentice system, which was central to the notion of craft unions. James Menzies, president of the Carriage and Mason Workers Union, expressed their views well:

> The men who are going to pay for those schools are the men who are going to suffer. Their boys of course will have an opportunity to learn a trade, but the trade will be no good. After they learned the trade they cannot go out and demand anything as there are too many men on the market.[9]

Some who were in favor of industrial education felt that it should not be the responsibility of the public school system. Charles Adams, one of these, asked, "Why should manufacturers shirk upon the public the instruction which can be in large part given better in their own shops?"[10]

Most of those testifying at the hearings agreed that industrial education was inevitable. The arguments instead centered around who should control it and pay for it. This debate was not only waged in Massachusetts. The backdrop for the Douglas Commission on Industrial Education was a national discussion on the problem of public education and the place of industrial education in the plan to transform the schools. The National Association of Manufacturers had been extolling the virtues of industrial education for some time, and in the same year, 1905, appointed its own Committee on Industrial Education. Its report concluded that "trade schools properly protected from the domination and withering blight of organized labor are the one and only remedy for the present intolerable conditions."[11]

Trade schools had become a weapon against the growing trade union movement, and the AFL fought back, con-

---

9) Ibid.

10) Ibid.

11) Lawrence Cremin, *The Transformation of the School: Progressivism in American Education, 1876–1957* (New York: Vintage Books, 1961), p. 38.

demning the manufacturers' support of industrial education at their 1905 convention. However, the AFL was a moderate craft union that accepted the employer-employee relationship as it existed. Unlike some of the more militant unions, its leaders were willing to work with manufacturers if agreement could be reached.

The Massachusetts Commission issued its report in 1906, one of the first states to come to terms with the problem. The commission was critical of the manual training programs that did exist. They did not adequately train for an industrial trade and placed too much emphasis on academic subjects. Thus the commission repudiated the older manual training model in which both shop and academic subjects were offered to all students regardless of their future vocational plans. The commission claimed that the public school system had become isolated from industrial society, and students were not receiving useful vocational training. The commission's recommendations were not much of a change from the past, however. High schools were to be the focus of the new curriculum of elective industrial courses. The curriculum was to be redesigned in a way to reflect industrial life, and evening classes and part-time day classes were recommended for students who were over age fourteen and working.

The most controversial recommendation was that the commission, which was to continue, would have the power to establish independent industrial schools. Public education in Massachusetts had a long tradition of local control, and local schoolboards rose up in opposition. The new focus of debate on issues of local control now obscured the controversy over the merits of manual versus academic or industrial education. When the commission as an independent institution was abolished in 1909, the focus of the debate returned to the impact of industrial education.

Once industrial education became an accepted strategy, many questions surfaced. What vocations should students be trained in? What kind of training was most valuable? What trades were most relevant in a rapidly changing industrial economy? What were the educational goals of these new programs? Schooling for job placement became the dominant trend in education in this period. *Relevance* was a key word that was increasingly defined as job preparation.

In order to implement these changes in the basic structure of the schools, a new level of categorization of students for future placement became necessary. Vocational education thus redefined equal educational opportunity to mean differentiated education and equality of opportunity "within the personal and social capacity" of the student. The rhetoric began to take on a note of predetermination as the children from working-class backgrounds were encouraged to follow industrial programs while those from middle-class families were encouraged to have professional aspirations. Prevocational education and guidance became selecting agencies in which children were slotted into their future roles in the job market.

By World War I, Boston had transformed its educational system. The American ideal of a common curriculum in which all children were taught the same principles and values had been drastically altered. As the school system grew in size and the population in the schools became varied in terms of class and ethnic background, a school system that reproduced the class structure seemed to become inevitable. This was not done with one act but rather by a series of developments in which industrial education was a late step in a process that had begun with quite different goals.

CHAPTER 6

*Progressivism on
the Wane: The
Entrenchment of
the Bureaucracy,
1900–1945*

SAM BARNES

Lewis Hine captures a Boston public school classroom in 1917.

Both the manual training and kindergarten movements eventually became part of the larger progressive pedagogy, but neither saw itself as part of this larger movement in its earliest days. Progressivism in education was a growing coalition of these more independent reform programs, such as manual and vocational education, which gained new vigor as they took on the shape of larger progressive reform that was gaining strength at the turn of the century.

Political reform in Boston began as a fairly overt anti-Irish activity. In 1888 when Irish-born Hugh O'Brien ran for his fourth term as mayor, he was defeated by a Yankee, Thomas Hart Norton. Initially these Yankee reformers merely wanted to retain their political power and to hold back the growing immigrant machines. Despite the fact that the majority of children in the schools were immigrant, the school committee members were Yankee. In order to keep the schools out of Irish hands, they initiated changes that altered the size and method of election of the school committee. In 1875 the school committee was reduced from 116 members elected by districts to 24 members elected at large. In this way, the Yankee population would maintain its control in a city that was increasingly becoming Irish. Four year later, women were given the right to vote in school committee elections. Both changes were aimed at reducing Irish power. The political machines had their strongest bases of support in the individual wards, and they were hard to challenge. Citywide, however, the reformers believed that they had a far better chance of capturing a majority of slots. Once enfranchised, Yankee women voted in larger numbers than their Irish-Catholic counterparts, again reinforcing the power of the older Bostonians in their struggle with the new arrivals and their descendants.

The initial impact of these changes was not as great as expected. In 1884 there was a Democratic sweep of the school committee, and as late as 1888 Roman Catholics held a significant number of seats. However, the reformers were not idle. In 1889 the Citizens Public School Union was founded to support the election of members to the Boston School Committee who were better qualified—in their opinion—than the incumbents. This union, often regarded as blatantly anti-Irish Catholic was superseded by the more moderate and more effective Public School Association in the mid-1890s. While many of the P.S.A.'s leaders were also linked with the Immigrant Restriction League, they were able to build a wide base of support around the reform of educational practices in Boston. The P.S.A.'s stated purpose was to maintain high standards in the administration of the schools. To do this, the association ran candidates of its own persuasion for the school committee with remarkable success. By 1902, sixteen of the twenty-four members of the Boston School Committee were there with P.S.A. backing. Most of these were upper-class Bostonians of Anglo-Saxon heritage who subscribed to the social reform ideology.

In the early years of the P.S.A., its primary emphasis was to keep the politicians out of the schools, to cut patronage, to make schools less expensive, and to make their administration more efficient. There was little talk of improving the curriculum or of making the classes more interesting, although certainly that was in some people's minds. By the turn of the twentieth century, however, a second generation of considerably broader minded Yankee reformers emerged who were concerned not only with consolidating their own shrinking power base but with genuine change in the quality of Boston's schools.

In the career of James Jackson Storrow, this second-generation Yankee reform style reached its peak. A Harvard graduate and promising Boston attorney, Storrow, fresh from his role in the rebuilding of the Charles River embankment, was enlisted by the Public School Association to run for the school committee in 1901. He won his three-year term handily and went on to use his position as a platform for municipal reform. Once he became an elected official, Storrow's Brahmin sense of public service was appalled at what he perceived to be the inefficiency and antiquated nature of the school administration. The school committee had twenty-four at-large members at this point, and the Irish political machine had made significant inroads. Storrow found the process frustrating and began to consider a reorganization of the committee.

The major accomplishment of Storrow's first term was

James Jackson Storrow, 1864–1926, Yankee reformer par excellence.

the opening of schools in poor neighborhoods in the afternoon and evening. He wrote: "Let the city make some effort to do something for the poorest of boys and girls; let the experiment be tried in opening the schoolhouse to them after school hours and of offering practical instruction, gymnastics, talks and discussion, or whatever else may attract them. Their parents, too, ought to be drawn by these evening opportunities to make the acquaintance of the teachers."[1] This commu-

1) Henry Greenleaf Pearson, *Son of New England: James Jackson Storrow, 1864–1926* (Boston: Thomas Todd Company, 1932), p. 47.

nity use of the schools for the children of the poor followed the settlement house model, which was thriving in Boston at this time. Storrow is typical of progressive reformers who felt that he and his class had a responsibility to educate and uplift the lower classes.

The structure of the school committee and the lack of efficiency continued to bother Storrow, who believed an efficient, businesslike, and professional system was needed. He approached the small Harvard School of Education to draft a plan for reorganizing the school committee. The charter reform that they put together reflected their Brahmin bias. They proposed that the school committee be reduced to five at-large members appointed by the mayor. They would have a policy-making function only; the administrative power would be in the hands of a professional staff.

The legislature, which must approve all charter changes, adopted the plan except for the method of choosing members. Because the committee was an important and powerful institution, they believed that the members should be elected. In 1905 the structure of the school committee was changed to its current one of five members, elected citywide. Storrow and the reformers hoped that this new smaller committee, with its professional staff, could keep the so-called politicians out.

Storrow ran for one of these five positions and was elected. The new school committee made some reforms: it introduced health services into the schools, expanded night schools, and founded the High School of Commerce and the Girls' High School of Practical Arts.

The next logical step for Storrow was to move to the city council and mayoral structures to push for more reforms. Following the pattern of consolidation of central administration, a second change in the city charter expanded the mayor's powers and extended the term of office to four years. Storrow ran for mayor in 1910 but was defeated by John F. Fitzgerald ("Honey Fitz"). Four years later James Michael Curley was elected mayor. The Yankee dominated progressive movement was no longer a decisive force in electoral politics.

Progressive reformers simply could not build a base in Boston. One historian gives this reason for their failure:

The reformers were asking them [the immigrants] to
vote for a government that would provide them with as
little as possible at the dispensation of experts and wise
men drawn from a class that had made clear in the past
its contempt for their capacity to be decent American
citizens. The sincere efforts of reformers such as Storrow and Filene to overcome the prejudices of the race
were fruitless in the face of the close ties of many members of the reform element to the Immigrant Restriction League and the memory of past abuse.[2]

For the next decade, the school committee turned its
focus to curriculum, pedagogy, and expenditures rather than
broader reforms because the basic structure and fundamental
purposes of public education in Boston had been established.
A small school committee, elected at large, was in place. An
educational program that differentiated between college-
bound and factory-bound students had been accepted.
Horace Mann's notion of a single school common to all had
been abandoned as American public education adapted to the
demands of twentieth-century industry and the reality of a
growing immigrant population.

Expansion of the schools in terms of population, program, and budget marked the period between 1910 and 1930.
Progressivism as a political movement was in decline, but
efforts at program development and curriculum reform,
despite their often limited successes, were important in terms
of furthering progressive education.

A major thrust of this movement was the development
of programs to meet the special needs of particular groups.
The earlier development of vocational education within the
public school system was a significant part of this aspect of
progressive reform. This trend continued as the public school
system set up intermediate schools, expanded its programs for
non-English speaking immigrants, developed one of the largest adult education programs in the country, and initiated a
program of extracurricular activities, which was copied by

---

2) Thomas Richard Mason, "Reform Politics in Boston: A Study of Ideology and
Social Change in Municipal Government" (Ph.D. diss., Harvard University,
1963), p. 355.

many other systems. The Special Commission on Education in 1919 emphasized this expanding curriculum in recommending "the organization of studies in high schools so as to meet the needs of all students and urging the general establishment of special schools for children who cannot read, write, or speak English, for backward students, and for feeble minded children."[3]

By the 1920s, Boston could boast many progressive reforms. In 1901 the elective system of courses had been set up in high schools. Evening schools were functioning well, and there were special schools for truants and open-air classrooms for children with tuberculosis. Testing and guidance programs had begun. The Department of Educational Investigation and Measurement was established in 1914. The following year, vocational guidance was formalized and a department was set up. Teacher training became more systematized. In 1919 the Special Commission on Education recommended that a state certification board be set up for teachers.

Although the period between 1920 and 1930 was one of growth in size, some programs stagnated. For example, teaching methods attached to child-centered education were abandoned. Control of the school department and school committee moved from Yankee to Irish, and school policy became more overtly politicized. School expenditures nearly tripled in this period, going from $7 million to $20 million between 1918 and 1928 while the number of pupils increased only from 107,000 to 129,000. The largest increases were in the higher grades, which offered more costly programs.

A key figure in this period was Jeremiah E. Burke, the superintendent of schools from 1921 to 1931.[4] Burke was first appointed to the Boston schools in 1904 as an assistant superintendent. Born in Maine of Irish Catholic parents, he came to Boston with ten years of experience as superintendent of schools in Lawrence, Massachusetts. He was first considered for the superintendent's job in 1906 but was defeated by a

---

3) *Report of the Special Commission on Education,* January 29, 1919, p. 18.

4) The material on Burke reflects the considerable research done on the subject by Sharlene Vest of Boston College. I would like to thank her for giving me access to her unpublished research.

Jeremiah E. Burke, Superintendent of Schools in Boston from 1921–1931, worked to develop the first intermediate schools in the system.

three-to-two vote. He continued to work as assistant superintendent and became most closely identified in this period with the effort to establish intermediate schools in Boston.

At the turn of the century, the system had eight years of elementary school and four of high school. There was an awareness that this organization did not provide for the particular needs and special problems of early adolescents. In addition, large numbers of students were leaving school between the ages of eleven and thirteen. They were not prepared for the world of work. The establishment of an intermediate or junior high school brought together several wings of the progressive education movement. The child-centered wing supported intermediate school as a way to respond to the needs of the child more effectively. And those supporting early vocational training backed the intermediate school as a way to train young immigrant children for their duties in the factory.

The intermediate school was first proposed in 1913 by Burke and was established in 1915. By 1920, it was an integral part of the unified school structure. Elementary school went to grade 6, intermediate to grade 9, and high school to grade 12. It was Burke's involvement in the creation of intermediate school that made him a logical choice for superintendent. He tried for the position again in 1918. Frank Thompson was chosen over Burke but died suddenly in 1921. The school committee appointed Burke as acting superintendent and then unanimously voted him for the permanent position.

Two other areas of reform were of particular interest to Burke and became more evident during his tenure as superintendent: teacher education and a curriculum in character education. Formal teacher education had begun in Boston with the one-year program at the Boston Normal School in 1852. In 1888 this was extended to one and a half years and in 1892 to two years. Men were allowed to enter the normal school in 1904, and entrance examinations were given for the first time. As part of the move toward standardization and efficiency, Storrow had introduced a merit system for teacher appointments in 1906. The course of study for teachers was extended to three years in 1913. In 1922, after Burke was appointed, the Boston Normal School began to grant B.Ed. and B.S. degrees in education after four years of study. In 1924 the name was changed to the Teachers College of the City of Boston and Master's degrees were granted. This increasing professionalization of the teaching force under Burke came after an effort by Boston's teachers to form a union in 1919.

By 1919 there were 3,500 teachers in the Boston school system, nearly 3,000 of them women, most of whom taught on the elementary level. The overwhelming majority of teachers

were products of the Boston Normal School who entered the
Boston school system as permanent substitutes upon gradua-
tion. For two years they maintained this status and earned
$500. Female teachers after this two-year apprenticeship
earned $690 a year. Male teachers, who were generally the
high school teachers and principals were on a different salary
scale; they earned $300 to $600 a year more. Female high
school teachers and principals were paid from $300 to $1,000
less per year than men doing the same job. The rationale for
the varying salary schedules was based on the premise that
men should earn more than women and that those teaching
in the higher grades should earn more than those teaching in
the lower grades.

In 1919, these low teacher wages were at issue. Teachers
had had no wage increases since before World War I, and the
rampant postwar inflation had severely diminished their standard of living. Their working conditions were becoming difficult in a growing bureaucracy where the mode of decision
making allowed for arbitrary authoritarianism. In addition,
the teachers were poorly organized, or perhaps over organized;
there were twenty-seven different teachers' clubs or organizations, some of them important, such as the Elementary Teachers Club representing 2,200 teachers, and others quite small.

Into this situation stepped the newly organized American Federation of Teachers, which had been founded in 1916.
The AFT developed out of the Chicago Federation of Teachers, which had been the first teacher organization in the
country to affiliate with organized labor. In 1902 Margaret
Haley, one of the founders of the Chicago Federation of
Teachers, focused on education as an important element in
the struggle between labor and business.

> Two ideals are struggling for supremacy in American
> life today. . . . One is that of commercialism, which
> subordinates the worker to the product and to the
> machine; the other, the ideal of democracy—the ideal
> of education, which places humanity above all
> machines and demands that all activity be the expres-
> sion of life. If the ideal of education is not carried over
> into the industrial field, then the ideal of commercial-
> ism will be carried over into the schools. Those two

ideals can no more continue to exist in American life together than our nation could have continued half-slave and half-free.[5]

1919 was a year of labor struggles, nationwide as well as in Boston. Telephone operators went out on strike in Boston, early in the year, and Boston police went out on strike in an effort to form a union which was affiliated with the American Federation of Labor.

Early in 1919 the American Federation of Teachers chartered Local 66, the Greater Boston Federation of Teachers, with jursidiction over all teachers in the metropolitan Boston area. This wide geographical jurisdiction was a mistake and created conflicts in terms of direction. The area the local was to represent was too wide for effective organizing, and city and suburban teachers had different needs. Another problem was the fact that only two of the seven charter members of Local 66 were Boston teachers. As a result, Boston teachers had a hard time believing that the union belonged to them.

Initially there was considerable support and enthusiasm for Local 66, but Boston newspapers immediately subjected their readers to an almost daily barrage of antiunion articles. The major focus was on exposing the organizers and charter members as having anti-American, pro-German sympathies, bolshevik, and IWW loyalties. This was a common tactic at the time, the nation was working up to the red scare of 1920. The initial error of the AFT in having only two Boston teachers as charter members also hurt the situation. These strong antiunion sentiments coupled with internal conflict in the union left Local 66 unable to mobilize Boston's teachers.

For a brief period of time, progressive pedagogy had some effect on the development of teacher training. The Teachers College of the City of Boston, which produced the majority of teachers for the Boston public schools, was headed by assistant superintendent Mary Mellyn, a progressive educator in the child-centered tradition. She had been appointed

---

5) Quoted in *The American Federation of Teachers, 1916–1961: A History of the Movement* by William Edward Eaton. Southern Illinois Univ. Press, Carbondale. 1975. p. 3.

by Frank Thompson, who had encouraged her to set up model
schools within the system where new methods and curriculum could be tried. Mellyn, a member of the Progressive Education Association, which had been founded in 1919, developed an elementary curriculum that emphasized a problem-solving approach with experimental exercises. She was responsible for writing the teacher promotional exams, which reflected her bias in educational methods. In 1923, two years after Burke became superintendent, Mellyn's direct influence over the supervision of teachers ended. Though Burke was open to child-centered education in a programmatic sense, he was uncomfortable with progressive teaching methods. Under Burke, Mellyn's power continued to decline. In 1929, she lost her responsibility for the promotional tests, and Boston public school teachers were no longer required even to be aware of progressive methodology.

Burke looked at character education as one of his major achievements. Having the same goal in some ways as the values education of the progressives, the approach and impact of character education was very different. Values education attempted to develop educated citizens by emphasizing the moral content in different situations. The focus was on increasing one's awareness of social relations and on the notion that one could respond differently to different situations. Values questions were encouraged in all subject areas and were not an isolated and separate curriculum. Burke's character education was a distinct curriculum taught for fifteen minutes a day on all grade levels. The style was exhortative, and the belief was that lists of worthy traits, stirring songs, and memory quotations would lead to good citizenship. More difficult questions of situational values were not recognized.

Burke's tenure from 1921 to 1931 can be viewed as a transitional period between progressivism and more conservative education programs, as well as the link between Yankee and Irish control of the schools. Before 1920 the Irish had made inroads into the political system. Beginning with Thompson and Burke, all suceeding superintendents were Irish. Burke was viewed as an educator, not an Irish politician like Curley. In many ways he was a bridge between the two styles; he was accepted by both the Irish and the Yankees.

Though the Irish had become dominant in terms of the school administration and teaching staffs, the school committee chairmen from 1906 to 1924 were supported by the Yankee Public School Association. For most of the 1920s, the political machines were not active in school politics. But in 1927, for the first time, the newspapers took on a school issue: the hiring of advisers for girls in high school at an annual cost of $25,000. At the same time it seemed that the pattern of politicians using election to the school committee as a political stepping stone had been established. A *Boston Post* editorial in 1927 urged support for candidates "who are committed, not just ambitious politicians intending to use the office as a springboard to more spectacular, lucrative posts. We need men with actual contact in the schools whose welfare is at stake."[6]

This election reflected the shift away from progressive reform and increased demands to cut back expenditures, which had risen so rapidly during the past decade. The new school committee of 1928 called for a survey to detail the expansion of the schools, particularly the burgeoning costs. The survey was an impressive document that detailed the growth of administration, personnel, departments, buildings, student body, and expenditures, but it was weak in terms of recommendations. The most touted one was the abolition of the schoolhouse commission, which was responsible for the building of schools. This was seen as a way to decrease costs and insure that there was less waste in the building of new schools.

In the preceding decade (1918–1928) forty-nine new schools had been built, including East Boston High, Trade School for Girls, Public Latin, Dorchester High for Boys, and Hyde Park High. Numerous additions had been added to older structures, and a new administration building had opened. Much of this construction went on when James Michael Curley was mayor. Curley, viewed as an Irish ideologue by most Brahmins, was known for the expansion of public works projects during his tenure. Viewed by some as ways to buy votes

6) *Boston Post*, December 12, 1921.

and support in Irish and immigrant neighborhoods, these parks, housing projects, and schools were often the first and usually the best services that had been provided for this constituency. In many ways, the problem was not that Curley had built too many schools but that there had been no assessment of needs, no projection of enrollments, and no attempts to see how each building could fit into an overall educational plan. In addition, there were numerous cases of delay or waste in the construction of the new buildings.

The city Finance Commission (FinCom) a state-appointed but city-funded commission was dissatisfied with the limited recommendations of the 1928 survey. Prompted by a new request from the school committee to spend $15 million more on construction, the FinCom set up its own committee to analyze the organization and administration of the Boston public schools. Using the data from the 1928 School Department survey, the FinCom report was much more critical of the school administration and made numerous recommendations focusing on the necessity of administrative control and fiscal monitoring.

In a letter to Mayor Curley in June 1931, the FinCom emphasized "that the principal weakness in our school system is diffusion of power."[7] It called for the abolition of the board of superintendents and the concentration of power in the superintendent's office. The report also called for assistant superintendents with assigned duties, who would be accountable to the superintendent.

Another problem was that school revenue was appropriated through nine different taxes. This method encouraged the expansion of spending, and there was no real way to monitor it. In addition, Boston had no system of gathering budget projections from individual schools, making it impossible to control overall spending. Administrative costs were growing out of proportion to the overall costs of education. In 1916 teachers' salaries took up 66.8 percent of the school dollar; in 1928 the figure had fallen to 55.6 percent. As new programs were introduced and new departments were added, the administrative staff kept increasing. FinCom thus recom-

---

7) Boston Finance Commission, *Reports* (1931), p. 93.

mended that the school committee have a legal right to appropriate a single sum.

FinCom also suggested many changes in the administration of the schools. Most of these centered around the centralization of power and the establishment of clear lines of authority. In addition, the FinCom report advocated a more complete budgeting process, which it hoped would reduce waste and overspending. All of these suggested changes were in the reform mold first initiated by Storrow in 1905 and they reflected the efficiency and corporatist wing of the progressive education movement.

Another area of concern to FinCom was the residency requirement for Boston teachers. FinCom argued that this reduced the quality of teaching in Boston and opened up the school system to political patronage. It recommended that this requirement be lifted, but as with most of the other recommendations, there was no response.

Very few changes were made in the Boston schools during the depression. Enrollment declined somewhat, and virtually no new schools were built after the boom of the 1920s. The administrative bureaucracy continued to grow. Fiscal and budget management were still unfamiliar concepts at the time of the next survey in 1944. The curriculum that had been developed fifteen to twenty years previously was still intact. It was so structured that at a given hour the same material was often presented in all given grade levels through the city.

The 1944 FinCom study of the schools was another attempt at reform that failed. George Strayer, a professor at Teachers College at Columbia University in New York City, was hired to head up the survey team. Unlike the 1931 survey, the Strayer report focused on the total educational program, not just administrative and fiscal problems.

The 1,700-page report came down hard on the Boston schools, citing many of the same issues that had been prominent in 1931. Strayer recommended a single administrator, with assistant superintendents who would have functional rather than geographic responsibilities. He reemphasized the need for a budget, citing Boston as one of the few school systems in the country lacking a budget process or overall financial plan. At this point, since enrollment was declining,

and many school buildings were old, closings were recommended, but not before an overall plan was prepared to project post-war enrollments and building needs.

Strayer called for a different method of election to the
school committee in an attempt to wrest power from the Irish
political machines. Claiming that his proposed method would
break the "political link" in which the school committee was
used as a springboard to higher office, Strayer proposed that
the election process be taken away from the voters and be
given to a "respected" body of citizens. This body, to be com-
posed of the chief justice of the Massachusetts Supreme
Court, and the presidents of the Boston Chamber of Commerce, the Home and School Association, the Boston Federation of Labor, the League of Women Voters, Boston College, Boston University, Harvard University, and Simmons
College, would nominate two people for each vacancy and
the mayor would then choose. Though this proposal was
developed to depoliticize the school committee, it was interpreted by many as a way to return the Boston Schools to the
Yankees.

The Strayer report called for many educational and
curriculum changes. Noting that Boston was a leader in early
reform, the report documented the decline in innovative
education in Boston and the lack of commitment to programs
such as guidance, that had originated in the city. In all
areas,—elementary, intermediate, and secondary school—
there was a need for new curriculum and materials. Some
programs, such as physical education and health education,
were not implemented system-wide. Adult education needed
to be revamped, and the kindergarten curriculum was considered dull and unstimulating.

Although Boston at one time had been a center for
educational reform and innovation, the system seemed to
have lost the ability and the commitment to carry out these
reforms. The bureaucracy that had been begun in the 1870s
was fully entrenched and had brought reform of the system to
a halt by the 1930s.

CHAPTER 7

Segregation and Desegregation in Boston's Schools, 1961–1974

HENRY L. ALLEN

Ellen Jackson, one of the inspirational leaders of the civil rights movement in Boston, and an organizer of Operation Exodus, addressing a group of supporters.

In 1855 the Massachusetts legislature enacted legislation banning segregated public education in the commonwealth. The law was the culmination of more than twenty-five years of protest by a large segment of Boston's black community and their abolitionist allies against the segregated public school system.

More than one hundred years later, in 1961, the NAACP in Boston claimed that there were at least six de facto segregated public schools in Boston and that black children were receiving an unequal and inferior education. Over the next thirteen years, the city once again focused on the battle to desegregate Boston's schools. The end result of that battle is well known; the United States District Court found, in June 1974, that the Boston School Committee had deliberately segregated the public schools. The context and history of that story is less well known.[1]

Between 1855 and the turn of the century, a majority of the black community was beginning to resettle in the South End and Lower Roxbury. Although the state law prohibiting desegregation was still in effect, there existed what was commonly referred to as the "colored school" in the South End. While Jim Crowism swept through the nation, Boston did not remain immune. The national rush away from equality and toward segregation had its impact in Boston. Segregation in jobs, housing, and schooling was spreading. A few black children occasionally gained admission to one of the city's few high schools, but for the most part black children were confined to their school.

There were protests against this new segregation. A leading spokesman was William Monroe Trotter, a black Bostonian in the tradition of the militant black abolitionists. For twenty-five years (1910–1934) Trotter, through his newspaper, the *Guardian,* preached and agitated against all forms of discrimination and for full equal rights for blacks whether in the south or in Boston's schools. In the 1930s a newly revived NAACP chapter in Boston demanded equality of educational

---

1) The author is indebted to Jim Green and Allen Hunter, editors of *Radical America* for their critically important essay, "Racism and Busing in Boston," 8:6, Nov.-Dec. 1974, pp. 1-32.

opportunity for black children in the public schools. But the isolation and size of Boston's black community, coupled with the absence of a national civil rights movement that could spur and support a school desegregation movement, led to the frustration and failure of these efforts.

As late as 1940, the black population of the city was less than 3 percent, numbering slightly more than 20,000. It was not until after World War II that the percentage and the absolute numbers significantly increased. In 1950, the numbers were 5 percent and 40,000; in 1960, 9 percent and 63,000; and by 1970 nearly 17 percent and over 100,000. Black migration to Boston was later and smaller than in many other northern urban centers, but the results were all too familiar. Discrimination in housing, employment, and education deepened and intensified as the black community grew and expanded.

This black immigration was occurring during the period that Boston's economy was generally declining, a long process that culminated in the fiscal crisis of the 1970s. With industry relocating, jobs being lost, tax revenues decreasing, city services being cut back, and the suburbs attracting middle-income residents, competition for scarce resources generated hostility and discrimination. What little advantage there was in this effort to secure jobs, housing, or good education usually rested with those who could count on political machines, patronage, segregated craft unions, and skin color.

The rise of the new Boston beginning in the mid-1950s led to developments that seriously undermined many of these advantages enjoyed by earlier generations of immigrants. Federal, state, and local policies and money led to new industry, housing, and transportation networks on the periphery of the cities. Neither the expanding black population in the city nor the vast majority of white working-class residents had access to these jobs or housing. Boston's financial community and its political leadership exacerbated these developments with solutions that benefited primarily themselves.

Massive urban-renewal schemes bulldozed entire neighborhoods to make way for luxury housing to lure the middle and upper classes back into the city. Downtown redevelopment led to new government, banking, insurance, and office buildings in an effort to revive Boston as a commercial and finance center. Huge tax breaks to real estate developers and owners used as inducements to build in Boston substantially increased the tax burden for older commercial property owners, as well as homeowners and tenants. Not nearly enough low- or moderate-income housing was built, or enough jobs created, to have much of a positive economic impact on the poor, black or white.

Economic stagnation, poor urban planning, and the desperate desire to retain whatever advantages there were to be had in this situation are part of the background to the depth and intensity of resistance that civil rights and school desegregation forces were to encounter as that movement began in the late 1950s and early 1960s. These problems were coupled with a general lack of political leadership and organization capable of turning mistrust, competition, and race prejudice, which constantly fueled these problems, into an understanding that the fate of poor and working people of all colors were indissolubly linked. Instead there emerged a movement committed to preserving inequality and segregation.

The Struggle Begins

In 1961 the NAACP concluded a study of the Boston public schools that documented the de facto segregation and unequal educational opportunity for black children. That report represented the first skirmish in a battle that was to last for the next thirteen years. It would have been very difficult to carry on that struggle were it not for two factors: the determination and commitment of the black community to equality of educational opportunity and the national civil rights movement, which had been growing across the south for several years. By the early 1960s, the North was discovering that, since the Supreme Court's 1954 *Brown* v. *Board of Education* decision, it was not immune to efforts aimed at eliminating racism and discrimination. Boston, which to many Americans retained a reputation for liberal race relations, became a major battlefield. If one had asked either the local NAACP leadership or the members of the Boston School Committee in 1961 if they expected such a situation to develop, the answer almost certainly would have been no. Yet it happened—and with an intensity and ferocity that startled many.

The NAACP study was scoffed at and even ridiculed by a surprisingly wide spectrum of public opinion. Even the newly created Massachusetts Commission Against Discrimination initially rejected the study's conclusions. The superintendent of schools, Frederick Gillis, rejected outright the NAACP's claims. He established a pattern of response that was to be followed by successive superintendents and school committees: there was no segregation in the Boston public schools and all children were receiving a quality education.

The local chapter of the NAACP decided to challenge this response with an electoral strategy, which it was to follow over the next several years. Through a combination of voter education and registration, to take advantage of the growing black population, and an effort to build coalitions with white, middle-class educational reformers, the NAACP hoped to mobilize public sentiment and support for desegregation. Appealing to conscience and common sense, the coalition would attempt to convince Boston's voters of the need for new leadership on the school committee to deal with both segregation and the poor quality of public school education. What probably could not be foreseen was the extent to which the issue of racism would dominate educational politics over the next fifteen years.

In three successive school committee elections—1961, 1963, and 1965—the reformers ran candidates endorsed by the Citizens for Boston's Schools. The organization's platform stressed the educational issues that they hoped would lead to victory: relieving overcrowded classrooms and buildings, building new schools, updating curriculum materials and teaching methods, instituting managerial reforms, and eliminating patronage. In addition, the reformers were pledged to respond to the concerns of the black community, most importantly, segregation.

The reformers were initially successful in electing two reform candidates in 1961, but only one—Arthur Gartland—remained committed to their program. As race became the dominant issue in each successive school committee election, both the black community and educational reformers suffered electoral defeats, culminating with the defeat of Gartland in 1965. The elections were intertwined with the escalating civil rights movement in the city. At the same time, politicians like Louise Day Hicks emerged to exploit the issue in election after election, insuring their own reelection as well as continued escalation and confrontation over school segregation. Hicks herself became both a local and national symbol of resistance to desegregation of public schools.

Electoral politics did not seem to offer much hope to the black community at that time. Sensing this reality, the NAACP decided to diversify its tactics. It demanded that the Boston School Committee hold public hearings to discuss de facto segregation in the schools. This demand was inspired and pushed by a new militancy growing in Boston under the leadership of young veterans of the civil rights struggles in the South. CORE, Boston Action Group, Northern Student Movement, and the Massachusetts Freedom Movement joined with the NAACP in its demand. Moreover they threatened that if a hearing were not granted, they would call for a boycott of the schools and other militant actions. Clearly these activists were disinclined to wait for election results every two years, and their activism would soon get its first test.

The school committee, under intense political pressure from a number of different directions, including the governor and the attorney general, agreed to a hearing in June 1963. The hearing revealed not only the contempt that the majority of the committee members held for those who spoke for the black children but also the apparent necessity for the militant activism being urged by some. The committee not only continued to deny the existence of any segregation in the Boston schools but also strongly defended the educational status quo. Shortcomings in the schools could be blamed only on those students who came to school unready and unprepared to work, claimed one committee member. With that kind of response, a Stay Out for Freedom Day was announced for June 18, the first boycott of the public schools protesting segregation since William Nell's call for one in 1849.

On that day nearly 9,000 black students boycotted

school to protest their segregated and unequal education. Following the pattern of similar school boycotts in the South, "freedom schools" were set up in churches and community agencies. Black history and culture, as well as discussions on why the boycott was taking place, dominated the curriculum for the day. For most students who attended the freedom schools, it was their first contact with many of the subjects being taught. For their parents and others who organized and supported the boycott, it was their first direct involvement in civil rights activity and civil disobedience. The boycott therefore indicated the seriousness of the issue in the black community and the fact that the attitude and actions of the school committee would not deter them.

As protests against school segregation accelerated, not only in the South but in a number of northern cities as well, there were efforts to coordinate a national school boycott. Combined with increasing civil rights activity in the South, such a boycott was aimed at securing federal civil rights legislation to implement the 1954 Supreme Court school desegregation case and to put increasing pressure on local authorities, such as the Boston School Committee.

On February 26, 1964, a second Stay Out for Freedom Day took place. This time nearly 20,000 students boycotted the schools, including a small number of sympathetic white students, mostly from suburban schools. Once again freedom schools were set up, and many black students probably came away from that experience having learned more about their own history in a few hours than in months and years of their regular schooling. Joined by hundreds of thousands of other students across the country, black students in Boston had taken part in one of the largest civil rights protests in the history of the country. The local and national success of the boycott seemed only to stiffen the resistance of the school committee, now under the leadership of Louise Day Hicks.

An incident at a small elementary school in Dorchester, the Christopher Gibson, was viewed as indicative of the response of the school committee. A young, white substitute teacher, Jonathan Kozol, was fired for teaching a poem by Langston Hughes, "Ballad of a Landlord," to his black students. The poem was not on the approved list of reading

materials, and the committee used this as their excuse for dis-
missing Kozol. Protests from parents who had begun to meet to discuss the abominable conditions at the school were ignored. Kozol later recounted his experiences at the school in his book, *Death at an Early Age,* regarded by many critics as a classic indictment of the effects of segregated education.

The response at the state level was different. In March 1964, the state's governor, Endicott Peabody, persuaded the state board of education to establish a commission to study racial imbalance, a euphemism for segregation, in school systems across the state. The board had previously been approached by the NAACP, without success. In the wake of the second school boycott, a twenty-one-member committee was appointed, which included businessmen, educators, politicians, and the archbishop of Boston, Richard Cardinal Cushing. Over the next year, the commission conducted the first racial census of the schools and studied the effects of racial imbalance.

In April 1965 the commission issued its report, *Because It Is Right Educationally,* in which it concluded that racial imbalance was harmful to both black and white students. The committee offered a number of detailed recommendations to relieve and reduce racial imbalance, all of which were immediately denounced by a majority of the Boston School Committee in language that left no doubt that they were intent on preserving the status quo and would fight any and all efforts at ending segregation. Hicks labeled the report a product of a "small band of racial agitators, non-native to Boston, and a few college radicals who have joined in the conspiracy to tell the people of Boston how to run their schools, their city and their lives."[2] Other members picked up on one of the recommendations of the report, busing, and began to lay the basis for the antibusing movement that was to emerge in Boston and in other cities some years later.

The report vindicated the protests of the black community over the previous four years. Specifically it identified forty-five racially imbalanced schools. If we compare this

---

2) *Boston Desegregation Project. The Desegregation Packet,* published by the Massachusetts Research Center (Boston, 1974), p. 3.

number to the six identified by the NAACP in 1961, it reflects not only the extensive growth in the black school-age population but also the fact that the school committee, while consistently denying the existence of segregated education in the Boston schools, was systematically instituting policies that furthered segregation.

The state's new governor, John Volpe, alarmed by both the response of the school committee and the demands of the black community, agreed prior to his election to act and quickly recommended legislative action that would outlaw segregated education. In August 1965 the Racial Imbalance Act became law in Massachusetts. But neither the school committee, which vowed to fight the law, nor the black community, which understood that the passage of the act did not guarantee rights, accepted the law as the end of the struggle over Boston's schools.

The new law gave the state board of education authority to require desegregation plans from the school committee and to withhold state funds if such plans were not carried out, but the Boston School Committee resisted. It succeeded in evading and defying the act for nine years through a combination of legal maneuvers and appeals, lengthy negotiations with state education officials, and apparent lack of aggressive action on the part of the state.

Meanwhile activity within the black community continued. That activity also took on a more grass-roots and diverse character. Up to this time, protests had centered on boycotts, elections, political pressure, and passage of the state law. Between 1965 and 1974, protests to secure desegregation would draw on these previously used tactics as well as the establishment of busing programs, community-controlled schools, a black student union, and a federal court suit.

In the fall of 1965, under the remarkable leadership of a black parent, Ellen Jackson, Operation Exodus began. It was an effort to relieve serious overcrowding in some black schools while at the same time achieving some desegregation. Taking advantage of an open enrollment policy, the parents and community supporters of Operation Exodus began to bus as many

as four hundred children a day.[3] At first they had to raise the
money for these efforts themselves. They held cake sales, can-
vassed, sought donations from small businesses, and donated
money themselves to finance the cost of the transportation on
a day-to-day basis. The depth of the black community's commitment to integration and a decent education for its children
is symbolized by the efforts of Operation Exodus, for the problems arising from fund raising, organization, and political
opposition to the program were immense.

The school committee and school department were
constantly erecting barriers to thwart the program. At a few

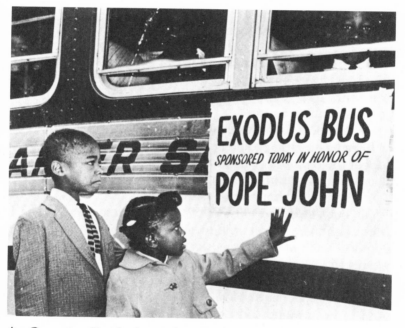

An Operation Exodus bus, taking black students from overcrowded
and rundown schools to other schools in nearby white neighborhoods. The beginning of the end for segregated schools in Boston.

---

3) There was an irony in this development. The open enrollment policy was instituted by the school committee as one method of relieving racial imbalance. Yet
when black parents attempted to use the policy, the school committee tried to
stop them.

schools principals locked their doors, claimed there were no empty seats, and then removed whatever vacant desks and chairs there might be. But since Exodus parents had school department figures pinpointing enrollments and vacancies, they were not easily dissuaded. School committee members railed against the program, claiming that children were being used as pawns in a political game and that schools were being disrupted by Exodus children.

Despite the difficulties, the program succeeded. At its peak, nearly eleven hundred students per day were being bused. Cultural, tutorial, and guidance programs were integrated into what began as an effort to relieve overcrowding. Exodus children were receiving an education they rarely experienced in their segregated schools.

The success of Exodus was critically important to the later history of desegregation efforts in the city. It was the first extensive grass-roots organization in the black community led by parents that had accomplished something significant in terms of desegregation and education. It had defied the Boston School Committee and won, and it had helped bring forth leadership that would be critical to the continuing struggle. For the next ten years its founders would continue to play key roles in sustaining the battle against segregated schools.

Another variation of busing that provided an option to a small but significant number of black children was METCO (Metropolitan Council on Educational Opportunity). Beginning in the fall of 1966, it bused children to suburban school systems that agreed to cooperate in the program. Ostensibly there were mutual benefits: black children gained access to educational systems that their parents viewed as superior to those in Boston and those same school systems were able to modestly integrate their overwhelmingly white student populations. Support services similar to those that developed in Exodus, cultural and tutorial programs, became an integral part of METCO. One critical difference between the two programs had to do with state funding, which METCO received from the beginning. Eventually a number of Exodus parents switched their children to METCO, and by 1968 Exodus ended its program. No doubt the combination of relief from constant money woes and the superior quality of many suburban school systems caused the switch.

A third option, which some black parents chose in order to improve their children's education, was the establishment of three alternative schools whose policies and programs, to varying degrees, were determined by the parents themselves. The community control movement, which was especially vigorous in New York City, took as its expression in Boston the founding of these schools. The total number of students served by the schools was a very small proportion of the total black student population in the city's schools. Yet these parent-run schools were as important to the black community as was Exodus or METCO, for they represented the ability of black parents to create viable alternatives that offered some hope of escape from the effects of segregated schooling.

The Roxbury Community School, the Highland Park Free School, and the New School for Children developed imaginative and creative educational programs. Parents were extensively involved in all aspects of the three schools' operations. An agenda of excellence was set for the students, many of whom excelled beyond whatever expectations the Boston schools had ever had for them. Parents understood that the critical difference was their involvement and control of the schools, coupled with an unshaken belief in the abilities of their children.

The community control movement, which was central to the school desegregation battles in other cities, notably New York, was a more limited phenomenon in Boston. While some of the rhetoric surfaced, the reality was confined to these three schools.

For the vast majority of black children and their parents who were untouched by these alternative schools or programs, there seemed to be no other choice than to continue to pressure the school committee and the state board of education. Their efforts took various forms: demands to hire black principals and teachers at predominantly black schools, support of another black school committee candidate in the 1971 and 1973 school committee elections, and the formation of the Black Student Union for high school students. The BSU, somewhat influenced by the ideology of black liberation and

120   nationalism, carried on a series of school boycotts, which reached their peak in the spring of 1971. They raised demands similar to those being voiced by black college students at the time, including the need for black teachers, black studies courses, and respect for black cultural expressions. The protests, boycotts, legislation, and experimentation that emerged from the black community during the 1960s, while very important in the development of a new consciousness and new leaders, seemed to have little impact on the Boston School Committee. Year after year, the committee continued to deny that Boston's schools were racially segregated.

Eleven years after the NAACP study of 1961 and seven years after the state's racial imbalance law, a group of black parents filed a complaint in federal district court (*Morgan et al. v. Boston School Committee*) alleging that all black children in the Boston schools were denied equal protection of the laws.

Following the Federal Court order desegregating Boston's schools in June of 1974, resistance to ending segregation intensified. Marches and demonstrations like this, led by Louise Day Hicks, were common.

They further contended that the Boston School Committee had deliberately segregated the schools. It was the first time that the school committee was formally accused of de jure segregation.

In answering the complaint, the school committee for the first time admitted the existence of de facto segregation. It argued that this was the result of neighborhood segregation, over which it claimed no control, and a constitutional neighborhood school policy, which allowed children to go to school in the neighborhoods where they lived. Further, it argued that over the past ten years, it had taken affirmative steps to ease school segregation, but it had been frustrated by factors beyond its control. The members admitted that of the 96,000 students in the Boston schools in 1971–1972, of whom 61 percent were white, 32 percent black, and 7 percent other minorities, 84 percent of the white students went to schools that were 80 percent or more white in their student composition, and 62 percent of the black students went to schools that were 70 percent or more black. In effect 80 percent of Boston's schools were segregated because they were out of line with the racial percentage of the school population as a whole. The question that the federal court had to answer was how and why this segregation had occurred.

In June 1974, nearly twenty-six months after the original complaint had been filed, Judge W. Arthur Garrity made his decision. He ruled that the Boston School Committee was guilty of deliberately segregating the public schools. He based his decision on the evidence that the plaintiffs' lawyers had presented in court: that in at least six specific areas the committee had set policy that resulted in a segregated system.

1. *Use of facilities and new structures.* The court found that the school committee had allowed some schools to become overcrowded while leaving others underutilized rather than transfer students, which would have resulted in desegregating some schools. The committee, it was found, even went to the expense of building portable classrooms in order to avoid transferring white students from overcrowded schools to schools that were black but had empty seats. And new school buildings built under the racial imbalance law, which required new construction to decrease segregation, were instead used

to increase segregation.

2. *Districting and redistricting.* In the drawing of district lines, which determine where a child would go to school, the court found that the committee had used these lines to preserve the maximum amount of segregation in some areas of the city. Even in school districts where there was more than one school, black and white children were assigned to different schools.

3. *Feeder patterns.* High school attendance was determined by the elementary or junior high school that fed into each high school. Again, the school committee developed feeder patterns ensuring that most of the high schools in the city had segregated student bodies.

4. *Open enrollment and controlled transfer.* This was the policy that Exodus parents had taken advantage of in 1965. Despite that, the court found that these policies were used primarily by white students to transfer out of schools that were becoming, or already were, predominantly black. Evidence of discrimination against black students' use of the policies was extensive.

5. *Faculty and staff.* In 1972–1973, there were only 231 black teachers out of a total of 4,243, or 5.4 percent of the total. The administrative staff of the system had an even lower percentage. Most of these black teachers and administrators were arbitrarily assigned to segregated schools by the school committee. More than 40 percent of the city's schools had never had a black teacher on a permanent basis.

6. *Examination and vocational schools and programs.* The city's three schools that admitted students by examination only were found to be between 84 percent and 93 percent white, while two vocational schools were 66 percent and 75 percent black. A number of vocational programs located in high schools around the city were also found to be segregated. The school committee argued that this was the result of merit, qualifications, and student interest. The court concluded, however, that these schools and programs, like the rest of the school system, were deliberately segregated.

For the black community and its allies, the previous thirteen years of protests were justified and vindicated. The court decision conclusively proved what the opponents of

This AP Wirephoto from September 8, 1975 was captioned, "Black students leave South Boston High School in their buses and escorted by police as opening day of Phase 2 of court-ordered desegregation came to a close Monday afternoon. About 80 black students were aboard the buses." What the caption does not tell is that the vast majority of Boston schools were peacefully desegregated.

124   school segregation had been asserting since 1961, and for the first time it appeared that the school committee would be forced to carry out desegregation plans in the fall of 1974. There would be more obstruction from the school committee, which gave aid and false hopes to an antibusing movement known as ROAR (Restore Our Alienated Rights). Members of the committee carried on ultimately futile court appeals while ROAR used both legal and illegal activities in an effort to obstruct desegregation. Some violence occurred at less than a dozen schools in September 1974, but more than 90 percent of Boston's schools were desegregated peacefully over the next three years. The segregated school system that had been so carefully constructed and vehemently defended was dismantled. The prospect of equal educational opportunity for Boston's black schoolchildren now seemed more of a reality than at any time since 1855.

EPILOGUE

Toward the Future

HENRY L. ALLEN

Members of the Citywide Parents Advisory Council meet with the Boston School Committee to demand a maximum of 26 students to any one classroom.

126 Two events of profound importance for the future of Boston's schools occurred in 1977. In June, over two hundred parent activists—elected members of local, district, and citywide councils established by the federal court's desegregation orders—met for two days in a Conference of the Councils. Their purpose was to review the progress of desegregation and educational reform in Boston's schools since 1974 and to set an agenda for further action. And in November, John D. O'Bryant became the first black elected to the Boston School Committee in the twentieth century. This had been an important political goal for Boston's black and liberal communities since the late 1950s and early 1960s. Its achievement in 1977 marked a turning point in the educational politics of the city.

The two events symbolize how much the schools and the city have changed since desegregation. Even the most astute political observers would not have predicted that out of the turmoil and occasional violence accompanying desegregation would emerge both a multiracial parents' movement and the solid victory of a black school committee candidate. Years of protest and organizing were behind these changes and the resulting progress. It appears that a solid basis for continued change and reform exists.

For more than a decade, racism had been a major factor in maintaining the educational and political status quo in Boston. After three years of integrated education and perceiving that no amount of protest was capable of turning the situation backward to reinstitute the old neighborhood school policy, most people in the city had come to accept the new political reality. In turn, this has led to a sharp decline in the politics of racial divisiveness, at least in relation to the schools. The parent councils and O'Bryant's campaign created opportunities for black, white, and other minorities to work together in larger numbers and with increasing effectiveness.

The parents' councils especially provided a structure where parents could discuss and act on issues of mutual concern. The councils have broad mandates based on specific court-ordered rights and responsibilities. These include access to school buildings and records; participation in selecting and evaluating administrative personnel at certain levels of the school system, including principals; the right to review and recommend changes in educational programs and students' activities; the responsibility to investigate and help resolve racial incidents; and the monitoring of special needs, vocational, and bilingual education. Additionally four years of day-to-day experiences with the school system have forced these councils to deal with every imaginable issue, from physical repairs of buildings, to preventing school closings, to demanding acceleration of staff desegregation.

John D. O'Bryant, the first black to serve on the Boston School Committee in the twentieth century, is sworn into office.

For most parents this experience has been rewarding and productive, if often frustrating. They have learned that change comes very slowly in the highly centralized and bureaucratic school system. Nevertheless they have gained self-confidence and understanding of how that system really works. They are not easily put off or co-opted. And their involvement has begun to break the stranglehold of the bureaucracy. It appears that the more parents directly experience the system, the more they develop the consciousness that the education of their children has suffered too long in the hands of politicians and professionals.

At the same time that the parents' councils were set up, the federal court order also mandated a number of reforms within the Boston school system. Among these reforms was the creation of a magnet school district, a school district defined not by geography but by the special resources for high quality education which would characterize its schools. The hope behind the magnet system was that a series of outstanding schools, spaced throughout the city, might attract significant numbers of both black and white students who would choose to register with them. The result would be the voluntary desegregation of certain schools, offering exceptional educational programs. While parents are still pressing the magnet schools to live up to their promised special quality of educational opportunity, the magnet system has created the hoped-for set of voluntarily integrated schools whose student bodies do reflect the racial breakdown of the public school students of the city as a whole.

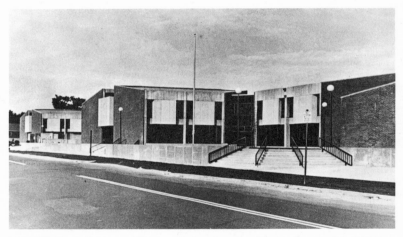

The William Monroe Trotter School in Roxbury. Opened in 1969 as one of the first magnet schools in the city on a voluntarily desegregated basis. It remains one of the best schools in the city.

While desegregation, the emerging parents' movement, and O'Bryant's victory have all had an important impact in changing the schools, it is really only a beginning. The question now is whether both desegregation and educa-

Scenes like this one represent the success of court ordered desegregation—bringing black, white, Hispanic, and Asian children together in the same classrooms and schools.

tional reform will continue their present forward momentum. In this context, parents and their allies in the city will have to overcome the limitations of earlier reform movements. Those generally acted to preserve the basic functions and purposes of public education without altering the power relationships governing public education. Except for the desegregation movement in the 1960s and 1970s, reform was generally imposed on the school system by business, political and educational leaders. Rarely in the history of public education in Boston have those most directly affected by the school system, the students and parents, had very much to say about reforming the schools.

To change those power relationships will require asking some important questions about the function and purpose of public education. Do the schools simply preserve the economic, political, and social status quo? Have the schools acted as a common melting pot to overcome class, racial, and ethnic divisions within American society, or have they perpetuated and distorted these differences? How much myth,

130   and how much reality, is there in the commonly held belief that public education offers the soundest guarantee for equal opportunity?

The answers to these questions have been debated in the past, and that debate continues today. The difference between then and now rests on who is asking the questions and who is attempting to answer them. It is not just academics, educational reformers, and politicians. Today those most vitally affected by the quality of public schools, in Boston and throughout the country are more directly confronting school systems and those who run them. Parents, community activists, and sometimes students realize that an understanding of their own experiences holds the key to unraveling what has always seemed so complex: the interrelationship between schools and society. The issues of race, class, and sex discrimination are historically interwoven in the evolution of the Boston public schools. Whether they remain so is the biggest question of all.

BOSTON'S COLONIAL AND REVOLUTIONARY EXPERIENCE, 1629–1819

Cremin, Lawrence A. *American Education: The Colonial Experience, 1607–1783.* New York: Harper and Row, 1970.

The first of three projected volumes in Lawrence Cremin's survey of the development of education in America, this book looks at the range of "agencies, formal and informal, [which] have shaped American thought, character, and sensibility." Cremin has focused his work not only on schools but also on households, churches, and the community itself as institutions of colonial education. This volume provides a useful survey of the background against which the Boston school system was emerging. Because of Boston's importance in colonial America, the city and the Bay State receive significant attention.

The New-England Primer Enlarged. For the More Easy Attaining the True Reading of English. To Which Is added, The Assembly of Divines Catechism. Edited by Paul Leicester Ford. New York: Dodd, Mead, 1897.

Going through many editions and small changes between its earliest publication in the 1680s and the American Revolution, this was the primary textbook of New England schools. In the *Primer*, Puritan youth learned the alphabet through a series of rhymes, the Ten Commandments, a few verses, and the basic statements of Puritan faith. A look at the *Primer* gives one a good sense of the basic beliefs of those who founded Boston's schools.

Morison, Samuel Eliot. *The Intellectual Life of Colonial New England.* Ithaca: Cornell University Press, 1956.

Originally given as a series of lectures in 1934, this book provides an excellent study of the founding of public grammar schools, as well as the other institutions of Puritan intellectual life from Morison's perspective. While his determination to rescue his Puritan ancestors from their bad reputation among early twentieth-century historians sometimes gives the book an overly devout tone, Morison's wit and charm make this a useful and enjoyable introduction to education in colonial Boston.

BLACK SCHOOLS IN WHITE BOSTON, 1800–1860

Daniels, John. *In Freedom's Birthplace: A Study of the Boston Negroes,* 1914; reprinted New York: Negro Universities Press, 1968.

A dated study filled with turn-of-the-century racial stereotypes, this book remains the most thorough examination of the history and sociology of Boston's black community up to World War I. Daniels, a student of Robert A. Woods at the South End Settlement House, made a careful analysis of existing conditions in the black communities in the South End and Roxbury between 1909 and 1914 and provided a good survey of black history for the preceding three hundred years. While the work includes little mention of schooling, it is important background reading for a study of the black experience in Boston's schools. The appendix includes an excellent brief statement of the integration struggle in the Boston public schools between 1800 and 1855.

Schultz, Stanley K. *The Culture Factory: Boston Public Schools, 1789–1860.* New York: Oxford University Press, 1973.

By far the best study to date of Boston's schools, Schultz's work provides a detailed—sometimes too detailed—account of the rise of the Boston system from the founding of the school committee in 1789 to the outbreak of the Civil War. Schultz argues that rather "than being a stepchild of European Enlightenment theory, or the offspring of domestic democratic trends in the age of the so-called 'common man,' the public school movement in the United States matured in response to what contemporaries viewed as an 'urban crisis.'" This crisis was especially acute in Boston whose population increased several times over as migrants from interior farms were drawn by the possibilities of urban indus-

trial jobs, and immigrants from Ireland sought to escape British rule and the potato famine. In response, the old elite
redesigned the schools to serve as the major institution of
assimilation and social control, indeed as a culture factory, for
those who were arriving in their city. The school system we
know today was the result.

Chapters 7 and 8 provide an excellent study of the rise
of separate black schools, initially funded by black parents,
after a series of petitions beginning in 1787 requesting schools
of some sort for black children were rejected by the legislature
and the school committee. These chapters recount the slow
struggle for the integration of blacks into the city system,
culminating in legislative action in 1855 that overturned
Judge Lemuel Shaw's separate-but-equal ruling of 1850.

REFORM, IMMIGRATION, AND BUREAUCRACY, 1820–1870

Cremin, Lawrence A. *The Republic and the School: Horace Mann on the Education of Free Men.* New York: Teachers College Press, 1957.

Cremin's selections from Horace Mann's twelve reports
as the first secretary of the Massachusetts Board of Education
(1837–1848) provide a thorough immersion in the public
rhetoric of this leader of the common school movement.
Mann's faith that the common school might "become the
most effective and benignant of all the forces of civilization"
provided the philosophical basis for the firm establishment of
Boston's schools in these decades, while his organizational
ability—and that of his allies—developed the system that
would soon have all the marks of modernity: bureaucracy,
compulsory attendance, and opposition to alternatives.

Katz, Michael B. *The Irony of Early School Reform: Educational Innovation in Mid-Nineteenth Century Massachusetts.* Cambridge: Harvard University Press, 1968.

Challenging the popular myth that public schools were
the result of "a rational, enlightened working class, led by
idealistic and humanitarian intellectuals, triumphantly wresting free public education from a selfish, wealthy elite and from

134   the bigoted proponents of orthodox religion," Katz argues that the emergence of the public school in early nineteenth-century America was much more the result of an old elite's attempt to control a newly emerging working class, made up predominantly of the large numbers of new immigrants arriving after 1840. Using case studies from Boston and elsewhere in Massachusetts—which makes the book especially useful to students of Boston's schools—Katz shows how thoroughly Massachusetts society was transformed between 1800 and 1860 by massive immigration and industrialization. The result, he argues, was that many no longer trusted the colonial network of family, church, community, and school to provide good citizens and turned to the public school as a useful institution for social control and assimilation.

_____. *Class, Bureaucracy, and Schools: The Illusion of Educational Change in America.* New York: Praeger Publishers, 1971.

     Continuing his analysis from his earlier book, *The Irony of Early School Reform,* Katz argues that by 1880 public schools had taken on the basic purpose and structure that would characterize them for a century. The purpose was an inculcation of attitudes that would reflect the dominant social and industrial values of the elite, and the structure was bureaucracy. The result was a school system that was "universal, tax-supported, free, compulsory, bureaucratic, racist, and class-biased." This book focuses especially on the struggle over bureaucracy within the Boston school system between 1850 and 1884, the years in which the first superintendent was fired, and the clear signs of a support bureaucracy developed, paralleled by a reduction of popular control from a large school board elected by districts to a small one elected at large and therefore more amenable to control by one social class.

Schultz, Stanley K. *The Culture Factory: Boston Public Schools, 1789–1860.* New York: Oxford University Press, 1973.

     This book, reviewed above, is of great importance for this period.

Handlin, Oscar. *Boston's Immigrants: A Study in Accultura-
tion.* Revised and enlarged. Cambridge: Harvard University
Press, 1959.

This book is helpful in situating the development of
Boston's schools within a larger historical context. A major
factor in public school growth in the nineteenth century was
the burgeoning immigrant population. Handlin focuses on
immigration to Boston from 1790 to 1850. Although he men-
tions various immigrant groups, the period is dominated by
the Irish migration, which he discusses in depth. Since the
early expansion of public schooling between 1820 and 1860
was in large part a response to the immigrant problem, it is
important to get a sense of what immigration actually meant
for Boston in that period.

Lord, Robert; Sexton, John; and Harrington, Edward.
History of the Archdiocese of Boston. 3 vols. Boston: Pilot Publishing Company, 1945.

This three-volume history of the archdiocese of
Boston, which was commissioned by the church, is the only
overview of the growth of the Catholic church and its institutions in the Boston area. The second volume, which covers
the period from 1825–1866, includes the history of the growing Irish population and the nativist response, which was
often violent. It also examines the early development of
Catholic institutions, including parochial schools. Volume 3
goes up to 1944 and covers the expansion and consolidation of
the parochial school system in the early twentieth century.

James Sanders of Richmond College on Staten Island,
is currently engaged in a study of Roman Catholics and education in Boston. This work will include the variety of responses
by Boston Catholics to educational issues, including the
founding and development of a parochial school system and
also the relationship of Catholics to the public schools. Nineteenth-century Boston Catholics, according to Professor

Sanders, had considerable ambivalence about schools; some vigorously supported parochial schools, but others were drawn to the city's public school system. When completed, this study will fill a major gap in our understanding of the educational history of Boston.

REFORM AND THE STRUGGLE FOR CONTROL, 1870–1900

Cremin, Lawrence A. *The Transformation of the School: Progressivism in American Education, 1876–1957.* New York: Alfred A. Knopf, 1961.

By far the most thorough study of the Progressive education movement, Cremin's book links the reform of the schools to the larger progressive movement, which transformed American politics at the turn of the twentieth century. While not specifically focused on Boston, Cremin's study is important because of the close links between Yankee-progressive attempts to regain control of all phases of Boston's life at the end of the nineteenth century and school reform struggles in the Hub.

Lazerson, Marvin. *The Origins of the Urban School: Public Education in Massachusetts, 1870–1915.* Cambridge: Harvard University Press, 1971.

Lazerson's book is a good resource on the development of public schools in the late nineteenth and early twentieth century. It is particularly useful in examining the political and ideological roots of the kindergarten movement, manual training, and vocational education. These movements began, in part, as a response to increased immigrant population and the demands of industrial economy. Lazerson also points out interesting connections between private philanthropy in Boston and educational reform.

Pearson, Henry Greenleaf. *Son of New England: James Jackson Storrow, 1846–1926.* Boston: Thomas Todd Company, 1932.

A totally uncritical biography of Boston's leading progressive reformer, Pearson's study still provides a wealth of information on the work and perspective of those who attempted, mostly without success, to reclaim control of the political and educational institutions of the city from the Irish political machines. As a leader in the move to centralize the schools in a five-member committee in 1905 and as a reform candidate for mayor against John F. Fitzgerald, Storrow spoke for the progressive trust in a professional bureaucracy over the rough and tumble of political decision making. As an officer of the investment firm of Lee, Higginson, and Company, Storrow also symbolized the much greater success of the progressive Yankees at increasing their control of Boston's economic institutions.

PROGRESSIVISM ON THE WANE: THE ENTRENCHMENT OF THE BUREAUCRACY, 1900–1960

Dinneen, Joseph. *The Purple Shamrock: The Honorable James Michael Curley of Boston.* New York: Norton, 1949.

Joe Dinneen was a political journalist who reported on Curley for many years, not always favorably. Curley was a major political figure in Boston for fifty years. From his first election to the common council in 1900 to his last term as mayor in 1949, he had a significant impact on Boston and its political institutions. He came to be the symbol of, and for, the Boston Irish in their conflict with the Boston Brahmins. Since that Yankee-Irish conflict was also played out in the Boston school system, the book is useful background for understanding Boston in the twentieth century, although there is little direct reference to school politics.

Survey Committee of Boston Public Schools. *Report of Certain Phases of the Boston School System,* School Document No. 12, 1929. Boston: City of Boston, 1930.

In 1929 the Boston School Board appointed a survey committee, which included the president of Harvard University, a judge, and a representative from the Chamber of Commerce, the Central Labor Council, the Home and School Association, and the school department. The purpose of the committee was to undertake an extensive investigation of various aspects of the Boston school system. The report is an important source of material on the public schools, much of it in the form of charts, graphs, and maps that detail developments from 1900 to 1929. Included is information on manual arts and training, vocational education, school buildings, school financing, teacher salaries, class sizes, and demographic studies of school populations. While many of the conclusions and recommendations of the committee are couched in terms of improving the quality of education, the fundamental purposes of the committee were related to fiscal economies due to rising school costs.

Krug, Edward A. *The Shaping of the American High School.* 2 vols. Madison: The University of Wisconsin Press, 1969.

This study of the forces that shaped and determined the nature, function, and purposes of the American high school is the most thorough and detailed work of its kind. Krug's study does not take a narrow view of education but rather puts it in the context of social, political, and economic developments. Krug clearly illustrates the conflicting values and ideologies of those who both supported and were suspicious of the emergence of the high school as a mass institution. The history of the high school is one in which all the forces surrounding the public education movement in America come into play.

SEGREGATION AND DESEGREGATION IN BOSTON'S SCHOOLS, 1961–1977

Bowles, Samuel, and Gintis, Herbert. *Schooling in Capitalist America.* New York: Basic Books, 1976.

Probably the most thorough economic analysis of American education yet available, *Schooling in Capitalist America* places the major reforms of education in the context of the larger demands of the nation's capitalist system. The research indicates little relationship between schooling and increased opportunity but rather a tendency of most school experiences to prepare people to accept an assigned place in the work force. Drawing especially on examples from Massachusetts, this book focuses on the rise of the common school, the progressive education movement, and the current changes in schools as reflecting the political and economic conflicts of the times. This is difficult but important reading for anyone who hopes to understand the problems of educational reform. The authors share John Dewey's faith that the schools can only become good when they reflect a larger society which is just; only a revolutionary transformation of the United States economy will truly reform the schools.

Garrity, W. Arthur. *The Boston School Decision.* Boston: Community Action Committee of Paperback Booksmith, 1974.

This is the full text of federal district court Judge W. Arthur Garrity's decision of June 21, 1974 (in *Tallulah Morgan et al.* v. *James W. Hennigan et al.*) in which he found that the Boston School Committee "had knowingly carried out a systematic program of segregation affecting all of the city's students, teachers, and school facilities and had intentionally brought about or maintained a dual school system." The court decision is an excellent starting point for an understanding of the issues of education and race in Boston during the 1960s and early 1970s. It clearly illustrates the politics of school segregation practiced by the Boston School Committee during this period.

Kozol, Jonathan. *Death at an Early Age.* Boston: Houghton Mifflin, 1967.

Kozol spent some months teaching at one of Boston's segregated elementary schools in 1964–1965. He was fired in the spring of 1965 for teaching a poem that was not on the approved list of reading materials, Langston Hughes's "Ballad of a Landlord." What happened to him and to his students during his few months at the school is the focus of the book. Kozol's personal experiences are a reflection of the racism and repression of the human spirit that pervaded the public schools of Boston, and most other urban areas as well. Kozol documents this with insight, honesty, and deep feeling. If we wanted one book to give us an understanding of the system as it affects its subjects, black and white schoolchildren, we need look no further. The events he describes transcend one class, one school, one school system, one time period.

140 **Lupo, Alan.** *Liberty's Chosen Home: The Politics of Violence in Boston.* Boston: Little, Brown, 1977.

Lupo's book is divided into two sections. The first, an examination of the political, ethnic, and racial history that led up to court-ordered desegregation, is a good summary of the political and economic struggles of contemporary Boston. The second part is a day-by-day account of phase one of the desegregation order and the crises surrounding it. Here Lupo is drawn into the momentum of the times and loses his perspective, which is the strength of the first half of the book. Still, it is a valuable work and an important account of the turmoil during the first year of desegregation in Boston.

Schrag, Peter. *Village School Downtown.* Boston: Beacon Press, 1967.

Another view of the Boston public school system, one that highlights its history and politics, is presented from the point of view of a journalist who spent more than a year visiting and researching the schools of Boston in 1965–1966. Whether Schrag is describing the school bureaucracy, the politicians who serve on the school committee, the schools, the teachers, what goes on in the classrooms, or any other aspect of the system, we are treated to a series of revelations about the schools that separates myth from reality and tells how the system often works. He enables us to perceive the fundamental conflict in values that set blacks and school reformers apart from those whose only stake was to preserve the status quo, at whatever cost to the schoolchildren of Boston.

United States Commission on Civil Rights. *Desegregating the Boston Public Schools: A Crisis in Civic Responsibility.* Washington, D.C.: United States Commission on Civil Rights, 1975.

One year after Boston's schools were ordered to desegregate, the commission held public hearings in Boston to assess phase one of the order and to help create a dialogue that would aid in the implementation of the second year of court-ordered desegregation. During the hearings, a wide variety of public officials and private citizens testified on the events leading up to and including the 1974 school year. This book is an often illuminating chronicle discussed by those who were in the middle of the events of that year. The commentary and analysis surrounding the testimony provide a fairly comprehensive view of Boston school desegregation. It also provides a basis for understanding much of the violence and continuing opposition to court-ordered desegregation.

_____.*Route 128: Boston's Road to Segregation.* Washington, D.C.: United States Commission on Civil Rights, 1974.

This study, which was compiled by the Massachusetts Advisory Committee to the Civil Rights Commission, is an important document on the post–World War II development of the suburbs and their impact on the city of Boston. In addition, there is a valuable historical chapter on black migration to Boston after 1945. Since the population shifts of the city have been greatly affected by the growth of the suburbs and the discrimination patterns that developed, this study is significant in developing an understanding of the current crisis in Boston.

ABOUT THE AUTHORS

James W. Fraser is a member of the faculty at Boston University School of Theology and a member of the ministry staff of the Church of the Covenant, Boston, and the First Presbyterian Church, East Boston.

Byron Rushing is director of the Museum of Afro American History, Boston.

James W. Sanders is a member of the faculty of the College of Staten Island, City University of New York.

Sam Barnes is an instructor at Bunker Hill Community College and on the staff of the Policy Training Center, Cambridge, Massachusetts. She has been active in the developing parent movement in Boston's schools.

Henry L. Allen is on the staff of the Boston Community School, and is a parent of two children in the Boston schools. He served for three years on the citywide Parent Advisory Council.